THE CRISIS OF DEVELOPMENT

THE RUSSELL C. LEFFINGWELL LECTURES, 1969

The Crisis of Development

Lester B. Pearson

Published for the

COUNCIL ON FOREIGN RELATIONS

by

PRAEGER PUBLISHERS
New York · Washington · London

PRAEGER PUBLISHERS
111 Fourth Avenue, New York, N.Y. 10003, U.S.A.
5, Cromwell Place, London S.W.7, England

Published in the United States of America in 1970
by Praeger Publishers, Inc.

Library of Congress Catalog Card Number: 76–115105

For a partial list of Council publications, see pages 115–17.

Printed in the United States of America

Contents

Foreword

As President of the Council on Foreign Relations from 1944 to 1946 and Chairman of its Board of Directors from 1946 to 1953, Russell C. Leffingwell provided creative and vigorous leadership during a period that was marked by a most constructive advance in the work and influence of the Council. It is in his memory that his daughter and son-in-law, Mr. and Mrs. Edward Pulling, and The Morgan Guaranty Trust Company have endowed a series of lectures to be given periodically at the Council by distinguished citizens from abroad on topics of major international significance.

The Council was honored to have this series of lectures inaugurated in November and December, 1969, by Lester B. Pearson, whose international statesmanship has been recognized with the award of the Nobel Peace Prize in 1957. Following upon his notable career as Foreign Minister and Prime Minister of Canada, he served as Chairman of the Commission on International Development, which, at the request of the World Bank, made a comprehensive and penetrating review of the problems of cooperation for development. The study offered interesting proposals for an effective global aid strategy in the 1970s and beyond.

Mr. Pearson chose as his topic "The Crisis of Development"—the slackening of the aid effort on the part of the well-to-do nations, and the explosive threat to peace and humanity from two-thirds of mankind remaining hungry, needy, disillusioned, and desperate. He addressed himself to the subject not as an economist or as an expert on economic growth but as "a practicing political scientist with some years of experience" and as "a citizen deeply concerned about problems of uneven and disjointed world development," with the incalculable effects on security and stability if they are not solved.

He has approached the manifold complexities of development assistance with insight and sensitivity, and he has presented, with realism and his usual eloquence, the case for international cooperation in attacking these problems.

JOHN J. McCLOY

THE CRISIS OF DEVELOPMENT

I

The Nature of the Problem

I have recently been the Chairman of the Commission on International Development. It consisted, apart from myself, of seven Commissioners who served in their personal capacities, without instructions of any kind from governments or from international organizations. One of these organizations is the World Bank which had asked us to inquire into the whole problem of international cooperation for development, the historical record, the present difficulties and the future prospects, the doubts of the developed nations and the difficulties of the developing ones.

My colleagues on the Commission, from various parts of the world, were, by experience and knowledge, extremely well qualified for the task. We also had the invaluable assistance of a small but highly competent international Secretariat.

Our work took the Commission to every continent, to discussions with people from almost every developing country and most of the developed. The Report which resulted from that work is an examination not only of where the development process has gone and how it got there, but also of where it could go now in the face of gathering difficulties.

It brings a message of hope in spite of difficulty, of optimism in spite of obstacles. But it is realistic. We know that cooperation for world development could accomplish great things for humanity. But we know also that it could end in frustration and discouragement and failure.

The Report of the Commission was submitted to the World Bank for transmission to governments and international agencies on October 1, 1969. It is therefore understandable that I, as its Chairman, should choose "The Crisis of Development" as the subject of these Russell C. Leffingwell Lectures. It is an honor to have been asked to give them. It is also a responsibility, the greater because I am no economist, development or otherwise, nor have I qualifications to deal with the technical or academic aspects of the subject. I am not even a social scientist! I think, however, I may claim to be a practicing political scientist with some years of experience. I am also a citizen deeply concerned about the problem of uneven and disjointed world development and the effect on the future of mankind if we fail to solve the problem in a way which will provide for social justice and economic opportunity for all people, and not merely for a rich minority.

The subject is a very broad as well as a very complicated one, and, in the time at my disposal, I shall be able to deal with it in only a broad and general way: the meaning of development, the historical background, the record of the past twenty years, the present aid and development situation, and the prospects for international cooperation in this field. Is it doomed to diminish and disappear with, as I see it, unhappy, even tragic consequences for the future?

In these lectures I will, of course, be primarily concerned with development in low-income countries, and with the other countries only in terms of their relationship to this process.

* * *

The low-income countries have been grouped in a category variously labeled "underdeveloped," "less developed" or "L.D.C.s," "developing," "poor," "aid-recipients." None of these terms is satisfactory, and some of them are misleading, with even offensive implications. This is due in part to the great differences in the countries that make up the low-income category, as well as to the difficulty in defining development itself.

The dividing line between the two categories of low-income and high-income countries is usually fixed at a national per capita income of about $500. There are, of course, borderline cases not easy to classify, and there are wide variations within both categories. Indeed, the gap between the lowest and highest in either group is wider than that between the top of the low-income category and the bottom of the other.

There are also wide variations among the developing countries in size and potential, as well as in social and economic organization. This variation, among other things, makes it impossible to apply common policies for development, or even a uniform pattern of aid, to the whole group —something that should not be forgotten in formulating plans for international cooperation or in establishing an aid relationship. If there is any subject where we should be careful not to generalize and dogmatize, this is it.

It may be said, however, that the great majority of the countries in Asia, Africa, and Latin America (the so-called Southern world) are separated from the others (the Northern world) by a wide and widening gap in income, in social and economic conditions, in the structure of production and distribution, and in demographic characteristics.

Today the per capita income of Asia's one and three-quarter billion population is about $100—about half as much as our *increase* last year on this continent.

U Thant put the situation bleakly when he said, "Half of those now living and two-thirds of those still to be born in this century face the prospect of malnutrition, poverty and despair"—unless, of course, we do something about it.

The low-income group comprises some hundred countries making up about two-thirds of the world's population. They are increasing in population much faster than the wealthier world—I shall have more to say about this later—while falling further behind in comparative income and production. The rich are getting richer, and the poor are getting poorer, and more babies, which some cynics claim to be the normal and natural condition of humanity.

I know, of course, that there is much more to development, either national or individual, than income and production. That is why nations which rightly pride themselves on their heritage of long civilization are naturally sensitive over being called "underdeveloped" or "less developed" or even "developing." It is nonsense, for instance, to conclude that one person—or one nation—is fifteen times happier or more developed than another because the ratio of income between them is fifteen to one. Development is more than dollars, and poverty is only one of its problems, though a vital one.

Nor is poverty an exact or even a comparable status. A farmer or worker in his cottage in a poor Asian country is likely to be more interested in how his position compares with what it was last year than in how it compares with that of somebody living in a high-rise tenement in a crowded city in North America, ten thousand miles away, where life may be "developed" in a way that might not appeal to him at all, let alone a way he should try to copy.

Nevertheless, as it simplifies matters to make classifications, however arbitrary, and define them, I propose to use such terms as "developing" for the under-$500-income category and "developed" for those above that level, realizing that many of the latter may be underdeveloped in other ways and that all of them are, or should be, developing.

* * *

What, then, do we mean by development? What are the obstacles to it today? What is international cooperation for development? Why is it so important?

In the purely economic sense, development is the process by which a state reaches the position where it can provide for its own growth without relying on special arrangements for the transfer of resources from other and richer countries— where its growth, in short, becomes self-sustaining on a reasonable level and may enable it, through its own efforts, to secure the benefits of industrial and technological progress for its people.

At the core of this kind of development is the effort to increase productivity and make it more efficient. Today this requires the application of modern science and technology, reasonable political stability, and efficient administration and organization. It involves all the techniques by which men now earn their living and produce their goods, especially their food. It means statistical services so that men can learn what they are doing—and not doing—and what they should be doing. It means education and trade and communications. It means a longer life, and a better one.

This leads to another question: Of what value is economic growth, however self-sustaining, without social progress if the increased wealth is not shared equitably among all the people and not merely among a powerful and selfish few? What is economic development worth if it is achieved at the expense of political freedom, or of that broadening participation of all citizens in national activity which we call democracy? Surely, growth, if it is to have real and enduring meaning, must also improve the quality, the excellence, of life for the mass of people, preserving those tested values and cherished traditions that do not interfere with the technological and scientific progress without which a country today is bound to be left behind in the march to a better, or at least a longer and easier, life. Social progress is also important in the narrower economic sense. In our own countries, without such progress, economic growth would not have been nearly so fast as it has been. Indeed, the modern mass-consumption market of our industrial high-income society is as much a product of progressive social policy as of wise economic policy.

Development ranges even wider than this. It means participation of people in the determination of their environment. It means the opportunity for people to choose and to use their resources to the maximum capacity. In the international context, it requires that rich countries, in addition to assisting the poorer ones directly, must be prepared to look at their own societies and see where their structure and organization are inconsistent with a good long-term global future and—this certainly is a counsel of perfection—make necessary changes in the general, not merely the national, interest.

The balance between social progress and economic growth is always a delicate one and can only be determined by the country concerned. However, if development is to be stable and healthy, there must be a more equitable distribution of wealth and a broader popular participation in political and economic life than is the case in some developing countries today. Without this, it will not be easy for people to make the effort and accept the sacrifices that will be required.

The record of the past two decades has been better on growth than on the distribution of its benefits. In many developing countries, increases in national income have been too highly concentrated in relatively few hands. Growth which merely makes the rich richer will not make for sound development.

Nor will economic growth itself solve social problems. Indeed, concentration on economic progress at the cost of everything else can sharpen and intensify social problems by preserving and even increasing disparities, which become less tolerable as the possibility of removing them develops. Moreover, traditional values and old foundations are weakened by the inevitable disruption that normally accompanies change.

While all this is true, nevertheless, with economic stagnation and no growth at all, there will be hopelessness, which one day will turn to anger and to conflict—if only the conflict of despair.

The next two decades, therefore, may require as much as, if not more than, the last two in the way of political and social as well as economic change in developing countries.

Restrictions on economic mobility and individual opportunity created by caste and class will have to be broken. Land reforms must be undertaken to provide incentives for future investment in agriculture and for increased production. There must be administrative reforms to make government machinery more responsive to popular need and more effective in implementing development plans. Tax structures must be organized to distribute the burden more equitably and to promote the collection of taxes without regard to political or personal status or economic power. Corporate laws must be amended to curb excessive concentration of power.

Unless these things are done, aid and cooperation for development are unlikely to show good results.

*   *   *

Development is, indeed, a many-sided process, even in its economic interpretation. It is also very different from what it was during the great period of Western growth in the last two centuries. It is, therefore, important to put development into historical perspective if we are to understand what has happened and what is happening. This is all the more necessary because, though the developing nations now have to make their way in a new and different kind of world, it is one based on a past when white and Western nations were concerned with serving their own interests in their overseas ventures, often at the expense of the indigenous inhabitants.

The process of modern economic development began with the peoples of Western Europe. Why should it have started there? First of all, Europeans acquired an instinct for self-government, rooted in the classical and Christian traditions.

This meant, for one thing, that the merchants in the great cities were able to achieve a measure of control over their economic and commercial activities—a control not achieved by the older societies of Asia, which were then the centers of wealth, creative arts, and skills. In Europe, the merchants and the cities and the corporations had opportunities for self-expression and self-management which were denied their fellows in other parts of the world.

Another factor was energy and enterprise—a desire for knowledge, curiosity if you like, which appears to have been deeply rooted from the beginning in the Western European world. An archetype of that world, from the Jewish tradition, was Job, who questioned God's ways with man; another, from the Greek tradition, was Prometheus, who was chained to the rock because he stole from the gods the fire which was the symbol of energy and which he wanted to apply to human needs and aspirations.

This thirst for knowledge and concern with its application, this creative energy born of curiosity, appear as a steady impulse in Western society. It explains why Leonardo da Vinci saw in mathematics both the secret of natural energy and the key to unlocking it for human use. The thrust began to reach a new level of power and influence in the eighteenth century, after European man had put behind him the theological struggles of the wars of religion and turned to natural science as a great field of human learning and opportunity, when men could find a new shared world of communication and dialogue and progress.

A third motivation was the desire for a richer life, which was the drive behind so many of the long sea journeys out to the trading East, to the riches of Cathay or the Indies. Behind these journeys, there was more at stake than trade.

There was the elaboration of financial systems, which became the precursor of today's business and credit structure. There was the growth of mercantile national rivalry, which pushed and sharpened political development.

Paradoxically, the source of this outgoing energy may have been the very backwardness and underdevelopment of Europe itself in earlier times. Europe was then a poor underendowed continent driven to move out and establish contact with other, richer and more sophisticated civilizations. That impulse carried European enterprise and vigor all around the world and, in doing so, elaborated new techniques of modern trade, commerce, and finance and began the process of modern economic development.

It also resulted—for good and evil—in a virtual economic take-over of the entire planet by men of white European stock. An appreciation of this process is essential to the understanding of where we are today; how Asian power became unable to withstand Western pressure; how the Europeans moved in and established their own commercial empires all over the world, which remained part of the Western system of control until 1945; how Europeans between 1600 and 1900 also occupied—if at times only as squatters—virtually all the vacant or semivacant temperate land in the world. Wherever the white man could go, he settled down and took over. In doing so, he developed the new land, opened up new resources, and laid the basis for the economic advances of the industrial revolution and for the technological, post-industrial society of today.

Until the eighteenth century, the bloodstream of capital for this expansion was basically gold or bullion or land, but, as the industrial revolution went forward, an important part of capital also came to be something called "credit."

This new instrument of growth depended upon men's belief that the methods they were introducing would, in fact, produce more goods for less input; that, therefore, in the future, money invested in growth could be paid back with interest. This belief in the new process of capital creation went forward swiftly in the West, though largely at the expense of Asian, African, and other overseas countries.

World trade was totally transformed in the process. In the eighteenth and nineteenth centuries the Westerners began to pay for the materials they brought back from Asia and Africa and the Americas with their new manufactures, thereby wiping out, incidentally, a large part of the handicraft and artisan industry of Asia, except in the one country which closed itself to European trade, Japan. The pattern of trade between the Atlantic center and what we now call the developing countries, based upon the exchange of raw materials for manufactures and capital from the West, dominated the world for two hundred years and, in fact, still dominates much of it to this day.

This, roughly, is how the cycle worked: From America or Britain or Europe would come the capital to open up a mine or establish a settlement or build a plantation. Then the raw materials would be shipped back. Any local development would be to facilitate this movement. Roads, railways, and ports were built, and the financial mechanisms for exchange created, all under the control of the Western nations and designed to help drain away the profits to them. Manufactures were sent to pay for the raw materials. These manufactures would be provided by European or American firms and distributed by the larger commercial agencies, all under Western control.

Only that limited sector of the colonial or overseas country which was concerned with noncompetitive and raw material exports was developed, or allowed to be developed. Very little capital or savings, so necessary for growth, spilled over into the local community. Whatever did, as wages, was then mopped up by the sale of manufactured goods from overseas, the profits from which went back to the metropolitan power.

Nor was this pattern easy to change. Over large parts of the world, colonial or dependent governments lasted until after World War II. In Latin America, while governments were no longer colonial in the political sense, many countries were held fast economically in their colonial or feudal inheritance, and some did little enough to escape from it by their own effort. Only Japan evaded the pattern and began, with hard and intelligent work, to build up local savings and invest them in local manufacture, while refusing to have open trade relations with the outside world.

Under these conditions it is not surprising that such development in the colonial world as there was did not lead to diversification, did not provide local savings or build an extensive local infrastructure, did not encourage local industrialization in competition with goods arriving from the Atlantic exporters. Nor is it surprising that, at the very end of the colonial period, the development situation throughout the colonial world was not much different from that which had existed in the eighteenth or nineteenth century, or that the basic facilities and energies for productive investment and growth were still absent.

Moreover, new difficulties in the way of industrial growth began to appear, arising, paradoxically, out of scientific and technological progress that had taken place, but which was confined to a few developed nations.

New techniques of production became much more complicated and roundabout than the old and customary processes. It does not take a man long to light and get heat from
a brushwood fire. But it takes a very long time to build a
nuclear power station. During the time the station is being
built, people have to be fed, workers have to be paid, and
materials have to be assembled. All this costs money and
takes years before the power station is providing electricity
and hence income. If somebody is not prepared to wait out
the process, to hold up his own purchases and provide the
finance without immediately getting a return for his money,
the power station cannot be built. Capital is what you pay
for waiting. But it's worth it, because at the end of the
waiting the amount of output that will come from your
nuclear power station, compared to the amount of output
that you get from the brushwood fire, is simply incom-
mensurate in every way.

To gain more for less thus depends upon being able to use
savings in order to pay for waiting. Before you can use the
savings, however, you have to secure them, and what chance
did colonial societies have for that?

They could save very little—not much more than was
needed for repair and maintenance work. Yet, if you are
going to have growth, the amount of savings in society must
increase and be invested. In fact, some economists have de-
fined the essence of development as the way in which a
society, which has normally been consuming 85 per cent to
90 per cent of all it produces, gets the proportion of consumption down to about 70 per cent and then devotes the
remaining 30 per cent to productive investment and to those
government services, such as education and welfare and
health, which are essential for the development process.

This reduction is not easy to make, for the very simple reason that nobody wants to have his income or his consumption cut back. If a government tries to transfer from consumption to savings a sizable part of the output of the community, it is likely to find a great many people either protesting or resisting, or both. Especially when incomes are low, people will bitterly protest at what they believe to be an attempt to lower them, even though the aim is to make larger incomes possible in the future. At best, it is a hard transfer to achieve, to accept present sacrifices for future gain. In fact, it is only tolerable when the over-all national income is going up while the transfer from consumption to saving is being made, when new resources are coming into being, or when new land is being opened up. Only under these circumstances is it possible to begin the transfer of wealth from consumption to saving without the desperate difficulties that arise when peoples' incomes are low and have to be pushed down further.

This was the inheritance which developing countries took into the postwar world, the world in which they are still struggling to find their way. It helps to explain not only how colonial societies fell behind in earlier years, but the complexity of the problems that face them now as independent states. It helps to explain also why in 1965 about 80 per cent of the world's wealth, trade, and investment was controlled by 20 per cent of the world's people living in the Atlantic area, with offshoots in Japan and Australia.

It is vital that we should understand how this situation, with its lopsidedness and its imbalance, deeply rooted in the patterns of colonial development of the last three centuries, has conditioned our world society today. It lies at the center of the problem of underdevelopment, a problem so complex

and difficult that one cannot help wondering if the 1970s
and 1980s of our century may lead, not to the kind of
growth and development for which we hope, but to a series
of interlocking difficulties and even disasters during which
all that has been done so far to build up the poorer parts of
our planet—and much has been done—will, in fact, be un-
dermined by a deepening inability to cope with crisis-ridden
local conditions.

We should never forget, in short, that the developing
peoples do not start from scratch in a new world but have
to change and grow and develop within a context unfavor-
able to them, because in the past their position has been so
largely determined by the interests of other nations. If we
forget this historical context, we will not understand the
problems that now exist; nor will development cooperation
to solve them be likely to succeed.

What a contrast to the experience of the Western industrialized countries, which I have briefly touched on! Here,
in the last two centuries or so, out of change with all its
inevitable turmoil there did come social and political as well
as economic progress. As the industrial revolution proceeded,
a technique, tolerable at least for that time, grew up for the
transfer of men and resources from agriculture to industry,
from the farm to the city. There were many abuses and
injustices in the transfer but on the whole it worked, at
least in an economic sense. There were an adaptability and a
flexibility that are lacking today. There were self-reinforcing
processes at work which helped cushion the shocks of change
that were bound to occur. There were new and empty
worlds across the seas, open to those who wished to leap
over the limitations of the old, and forty million from
Europe made the leap in the nineteenth century.

Today, however, with the conditions that exist in agriculture and industry, with "bigness" the goal of nearly all activity, with business and finance organized in monster corporate structures, with unprecedented growth in population and unplanned urbanization, with the dislocation and disruption that change and growth nearly always bring, development is bound to be far more complex and confused than it was a hundred years ago. The problems are far greater, creating frustrations and tensions and violence. This is especially the case where the political, social, and economic organization of developing countries—most of them newly independent—are not often geared to sustain growth, or to solve the problems that come from it.

Today great regions of the world are reaching the point of transition between the immemorial pursuit of old patterns of life and new and far-reaching commitments to modernization, industrialization, and urban living, which so easily create conditions of upheaval, of revolutionary disturbance, of fear and violence. Let there be no doubt about it. The next decade will, in Lincoln's words, be "piled high with difficulty." We are in an era of swift and often violent change. Doubts and fears and vast dissatisfactions surge up in the developing world.

*   *   *

The combination of rocketing growth in population and relative stagnation in the countryside has profoundly affected the whole urban-industrial prospect of the poorer countries. So vast a movement of people to the cities has been set in motion that, on present projections, if the developing world is to house and employ its migrant masses, it will need to build in the next decade the equivalent of all the city in-

stallations built in developed lands over the last two centuries. This is the measure of the uprooting, of the massive
growth and transfer of populations that is taking place.

And what do the migrants find as they move to urban life?
Houses? Schools? Above all, jobs? For millions upon millions, the misery they leave behind in depressed and stagnant
countrysides they find again in the slums and shanty towns
of the developing megalopolis. There is little likelihood that
these new urban masses can have a decent life unless there is
a massive international effort by the richer and developed
countries to help the governments of developing countries in
their efforts to make it possible.

I know that there have been encouraging changes in agricultural production in some areas. The Green Revolution
is exciting and important. It will give some years of grace in
which to achieve a better balance of population and resources in the countries concerned. But these changes have
also brought social and economic problems as well as triumphs in production. Because they involve rural unemployment as machines displace men, they are bound to involve a
transfer of labor, of men and resources, from agriculture to
industry, from the farm to the city. Yet it becomes increasingly difficult to make this transfer without dangerous dis-
locations. There will be more "landless men on the fringe of
the villages and jobless men on the fringe of the cities," with
masses of "hangers-on" living on the edge of despair and
destitution; there will be political instability, or worse, and
a climate of society which will make steady and balanced
development very difficult.

Furthermore, for sound and stable development, along
with increased agricultural production, there must be reform
which establishes the cultivator as owner of the land and

gives him a necessary supporting framework of cooperative credit, marketing and supply facilities, as well as maximum employment on the land. The model for the agricultural organization of the developing world should not be nineteenth-century East Prussia but nineteenth-century Denmark, with its cooperatives, folk high schools, and widespread distribution of income and opportunity.

Agriculture may well be the key to sound and stable development, but with progress in this sector there must also go "creative urbanization." By this I mean the planned development of more local urban centers, as nodes of regional growth and as creators of jobs for displaced farm workers, to prevent the huddling together of masses of millions in one or two great cities.

The population explosion, which I have referred to parenthetically, complicates and intensifies all other problems. It goes far beyond anything ever experienced before. At current rates of growth, the world's population of three and one-half billion today will double by the end of the century.

Moreover, the population explosion is much greater in developing countries, not because of an increase in the birth rate, which has remained constant during the last sixty years, but because of a decrease in the death rate from 28 to 15 per 1,000 births. More children survive; more people grow older.

Over the last fifteen years, newly independent India has had to feed, clothe, and find shelter for 150 million additional people, a number equal to the entire population of the United States at the end of World War II.

From 1920 to 1960 there was a world increase in rural population of half a billion. All but 56 million of this increase was in developing countries where there was not enough suitable land to support the additional people.

During the same period, urban population went up from 68 million to 320 million, half of which was in cities over 500,000; and, again, most of it occurred in developing countries. By 1980 the developing countries are likely to add to their urban population alone, more than the total population today of all the developed countries. Great metropolitan agglomerations have far outgrown the local resources which once sustained urban centers of regional activity and development. Today in Latin America, in sixteen out of twenty states, more than half the urban population lives in the capital city.

The low-income countries are not planned or organized to take care of this kind of increase, to manage this kind of development. Indeed the population explosion has taken place far in advance of most of the changes required for development, ahead of modern, efficient administration, ahead of technology and its application to modern industry and agriculture, ahead of financial and market institutions.

Governments of developing countries are now conscious of the magnitude and importance of the population problem and, with few exceptions, are beginning to give policies dealing with it high priority. They realize that, as death control has, fortunately, become more effective, some form of birth control must be produced as a counterbalance. Thus government after government is providing in its health policy for services which enable parents to choose the number of children that they will have; it is encouraging them to choose smaller families and doing everything possible within the limits of parental choice to make that choice effective. This is something new and very important.

If, for instance, we look at population control in India, we discover that a very small sum was devoted to it in the Second Five-Year Plan; the amount was doubled in the third Plan, and is now five or six times what it was in the beginning. Although not yet adequate, population planning in India is now on a scale which does begin to cope with the problem by taking the message of responsible parenthood to the half a million villages where the bulk of the Indian population lives. While it remains a fearsome problem, and one concerned with the most delicate moral, cultural and religious instincts of people, new population policies are at least beginning to have some effect.

Yet one might despair if it were not for the fact that population growth is more or less stable in Europe, in North America, and Japan; that in some countries of Asia, such as Taiwan and Korea, it has started to level off. If no country had ever achieved any form of population control, then of course we would have real grounds for despair. But this is not the case.

Also it must be remembered that economic development itself helps to bring down the rate of population increase because parents with wider horizons, better education, and more opportunity begin to want to have smaller families. Population planning, of course, must be pushed as a matter of urgency because economic forces take time to work—and we may not have enough time. But population planning must be considered as part of the whole strategy of development which will bring better life for families, better opportunities, better education, better health, and more hope. In such a context, family stabilization itself will be enormously facilitated. If we don't have this kind of development, people in despair may not care whether they have large families or not. "What difference does it make?" could be their reaction.

As we talk about the problems of underdevelopment—so pressing, so complicated—it is ironic to recall that some countries are economically underdeveloped now because they were overdeveloped in the past through short-sighted, un-planned, and wasteful use of their resources. Babylon, Egypt, Macedonia, Persia, Ghana, Mali, Guatemala, Yucatan, the Indus Valley, all were once rich, productive areas, exploited till they became eroded. Here is a lesson for us. Could it happen to the modern, industrial societies of today? Of course, and it will if we forget—as we seem to be doing—that technological and scientific advance, economic develop-ment if you like, is not an end in itself, but only to be justified and pursued when it contributes to a better and richer life for people in an environment in which such a life is possible. Progress can be made useless and even dan-gerous by short-sighted, wasteful, and damaging methods of exploiting nature's resources and polluting the environ-ment. This kind of development can lead to decay and death.

At present, our Western economic development seems to be based on immense consumption, planned obsolescence, and the maximum dissipation of resources and energies. When that intrepid voyager, Thor Heyerdahl, crossed the South Pacific fifteen years ago, he found it shining and clear from coast to coast. On his recent journey across the "devel-oped" Atlantic, he reports refuse, bilge, and broken bottles all the way.

The implications of flouting ecological balances are, how-ever, creeping up on us and, at last, entering into our consciousness. They supply a major reason why developed and developing societies alike, have to find a better method of living together on this planet. Let me give you just one example. It has been stated that if the degree of motorization which has been reached in the North Atlantic countries were to spread to all the other continents, and if world population were to rise to between seven and eight billion, the heating-up of the whole atmosphere of our planet would be such that we might melt the polar ice-cap. This, of course, would solve the problems of motorization, and everything else, as both Europe and North America would be under twelve to twenty feet of water!

Does this imply that if we of the affluent West continue our own way of life at present levels of consumption and waste and pollution, we must rely on all the other peoples of the world to live in a far more plain and simple fashion so that we can continue this "rake's progress" without early disaster? Are we helping other peoples by transferring our technology and our science to them before we have learned to control their application to our own societies?

What are we seeking to transfer? A system where man has become so overdeveloped technologically that he is decaying socially and morally, and is in danger of being lost in the imbalance of nature that he has created? In 1968, at a UNESCO conference, 200 experts from 50 countries came to the conclusion that life, as things are going at present, would in twenty years show definite signs of succumbing to pollution. Air would show the first signs of becoming unbreathable for man and plant, and lakes and rivers would no longer support life for any creature.

The fact is that man, restlessly probing and interfering, has dangerously ignored and flouted the laws of nature which control all life, and which have been so ordered that all forms of life can coexist in harmony and interdependent creativity. We should, therefore, think of mankind more as a society of gardeners rather than one of engineers, because in such a society we are apt to cooperate more closely with nature.

Man in more primitive societies could only survive when he was able to come to terms with nature. Are industrial societies now making this impossible? And is this what we wish to encourage in new, developing societies? Are we transferring our polluted environment with our interest-free loans and our technical assistance? What kind of "gap" are we seeking to remove? We have already ensured that developing man, however remote, should have his equal share of radiation in the atmosphere as a result of nuclear bomb experiments. There is no gap here. Even more important, we have arranged things so that if there is all-out nuclear war between the superatomic powers, all will have an equal share in extinction. There is no gap here.

No wonder there are some cynics who plead that the highly developed technological and scientific "supermen" should leave the others alone. But it is already too late for that. Such being the case, Asians and Africans, understandably, wish to share in our telephones, our airplanes, our color TVs, our medical and dental clinics, as well as, perforce, in the effect of other and destructive manifestations of technological progress.

Forty years ago, John Maynard Keynes indulged in another form of pessimistic speculation on the results of economic development. Thinking only about the West, though his thoughts are equally relevant to others, he wondered whether the solution of economic problems would not deprive man of his traditional purpose, as well as his most pressing problem, the struggle for subsistence. Keynes then asks:

> Will this be a benefit? If one believes at all in the real values of life, the prospect at least opens up the possibility of benefit. Yet I think with dread of the readjustment of the habits and instincts of the ordinary man, bred into him for countless generations, which he may be asked to discard within a few decades. . . .
>
> Thus for the first time since his creation man will be faced with his real, his permanent problem—how to use his freedom from pressing economic cares, how to occupy his leisure, which science and compound interest will have won for him, to live wisely and agreeably and well.*

Keynes would not have his doubts removed on being told that by the year 2000 A.D. the average income for Americans will exceed $10,000 a year, secured by a productivity which will require him to work only three hours a day. Recreation and ease will be the normal occupation, with work an interruption and "getting ahead" unnatural. There will be mechanical servants for everyone. Everything will be easy and permissive; no need for aspiration, ambition, and achievement.

This sounds like fantasy—perhaps it is. But as we insist on the necessity for development we should ponder over these things. Certainly we should not forget that the pollution of our environment, if slower, is quite as sure a method of global suicide as nuclear destruction. Indeed, there may be as much danger to humanity in the overdevelopment of rich industrial and technological societies, in the name of progress, as there is from the underdevelopment of poorer ones.

* Essays in Persuasion (New York: Harcourt, Brace, 1932), pp. 366, 367.

Therefore, the questions that face us are not only whether the rich countries should help developing countries, or how much help they should give, but also what kind of help and for what purpose. What values—and standards—should we seek to transfer to "developing" countries from our "developed" civilization along with our capital and know-how?

Many of our own people, especially young people, are questioning and even rejecting many of these current values and standards as inadequate and irrelevant to the requirements of the new technological society. Many are rebelling against technological progress itself as destroying real values, as something whose slogans, and much of whose substance, has lost its appeal. It doesn't "satisfy."

So why should we expect Asians and Africans to be enchanted with everything we label progress and development? They accept Western industrial superiority. They envy us our technical achievements and admit their value, indeed their necessity, for so many constructive purposes.

They don't accept Western superiority, however, in everything. In washing-machines, yes; but not in wisdom. In motor cars, yes; but not in morality.

They do not worship our graven images with loud hosannahs merely because these can perform mechanically all the functions that man once performed with his own mind and muscle. Nor should we expect them to. We should cultivate a decent humility and a sense of proportion as we rejoice over our technological triumphs.

I know that the developed countries, and especially the United States, have made an unprecedented transfer of resources to poorer countries and that this has greatly helped countries that needed help. In doing this, however, we have nothing to be smug and self-righteous about. Nor should we be too critical when some aid is wrongly used or when results seem to be slow or nonexistent. We aren't managing change too successfully in our own countries. We shouldn't expect new and inexperienced nations to do so without great difficulty.

We ask old but poor societies not only to modernize their methods and their institutions, but, in doing so, to abandon certain social ideas and values which have meant much to them over the ages and are deeply ingrained in their lives and habits; they can't be changed easily or quickly without trouble. And what do we offer as a replacement? Higher incomes and material standards of living, of course, and that is good. But at times, also, a form of life based on Western social and moral standards and values which are under violent and persistent attack in the West itself. It is wise for us to remind ourselves of these things as we seek to cooperate with the developing world.

The countries of that world should accept, as they do accept, the fact that they have to rely on themselves for progress. They hope and expect, however, that the developed countries will help them to help themselves to go forward.

Why should we do this? How should we do it? What are the results already achieved by international cooperation for development and what remains to be done? These are matters I will consider in the following lectures.

II

The Case for Cooperation

How should the rich and developed nations face the increasingly dangerous division of the world between the affluent and the needy, between the one-third who collectively have so much and the two-thirds who have so little? By their wealth and power, by the predominance they have inherited and still command, the rich nations will largely determine the pattern and progress of world development over the next thirty years. If they turn away from cooperation for such development, it is unlikely that it will take place in any tolerable period of time, or that we shall reach the next century in a world society that will be recognizably "human."

Indeed, there is no greater threat to humanity, no greater danger to peace than that from two-thirds of mankind remaining hungry, disillusioned, and desperate. Therefore, those who enjoy the greatest capacity, who have already crossed the threshold of economic development, carry a heavy responsibility. Even though the main burden rests—and must rest—on the governments and peoples of the developing countries themselves, their success, I repeat, will depend to a large extent on what the rich are prepared to do to help.

The commitment for cooperation has been accepted in principle and has been followed in practice by a massive transfer of resources from developed to developing countries over the last twenty years. For the first time in human history, rich and powerful countries have acknowledged an obligation to foster the development of poorer and weaker countries.

It is true that in the past, aid has been given by an imperial power to its colonies, and to independent countries for political advantage or commercial gain. Support has been bought, and governments have been bribed. Disaster relief has been given, and charity has gone hand in hand with missionary and humanitarian zeal. In the last two decades, however, while admittedly some aid has been given for political, strategic, and commercial reasons, there has been an official flow of resources, amounting to perhaps $50 billion, for the declared purpose of assisting the economic growth of poor and low-income countries. The importance and the magnitude of this effort should not be depreciated.

The fact remains, however, that the "aid effort" is now slackening, at least among the larger donors, notably the United States of America, which is by far the most important because of its wealth and strength. There is a "weariness in well-doing."

There is also some disenchantment in both developed and developing countries with the whole idea of aid and international cooperation for development. There are those who would abandon the business entirely and others who reject it as it is now carried on.

This mood is the more discouraging because it contrasts so sharply with earlier hopes in both developing and developed countries. It may be—as I believe it to be—unwarranted and unfortunate, but the mood exists. It is a major reason why we should answer the basic question: Why aid at all? Why should the rich and powerful states, beset by new and old domestic problems of their own and burdened with the mounting costs of trying to solve them, to say nothing about staggering expenditures for defense, feel any obligation to help other countries? Who should be surprised if the American taxpayer groans: "Guns, butter, outer space. All this and aid for two-thirds of the population of the world, and at a time when nearly every country greets our 'aid' with a banner, 'Yankee, go home.' It is too much."

These are the questions that must be dealt with if any part of a country's gross national product (GNP) is to go into foreign aid and development programs. They are questions that go right to the root of the present weakening of the will to continue, let alone strengthen, development cooperation, particularly in the United States of America.

It would be comforting to think that the experience of twenty years of world cooperation for development has been such that no further argument for aid is needed. Unfortunately, such is not the case. That there is a commitment for strong countries to help weaker ones is not a proposition that gains either easy or automatic acceptance. It is based on a recognition of duty that only those already convinced may find instantly persuasive.

*   *   *

It might be easier to secure general and firm acceptance for a commitment to aid if it could be shown that failure to give it and carry it out would produce catastrophic and immediate consequences. This is not the case, however, even though the ultimate results of failure could be tragic.

The argument that there will be "fire and brimstone" tomorrow if development cooperation ends today is not effective in the way that the argument of "total destruction once nuclear bombs begin to fall" is. Nor is it possible to paint a convincing picture of mass upheaval and general chaos, because we know that this will not happen—immediately.

In the absence of this kind of fear-inspiring, apocalyptic pressure, we dare not assume that abandonment of the development cooperation front cannot happen next year. It can. It is quite conceivable that the rich, white, Western nations might turn their backs on the developing world in so far as official aid is concerned in the belief that they can live with the resulting situation, at least for a long time. After all, these countries are poor and relatively weak. They have no nuclear weapons—or even napalm—yet.

It is therefore essential to make the case for aid and for development cooperation strong and convincing. The first part of the case is simple.

There is a moral obligation to assist. It is part of the higher nature of man to help those who need help. It is only right for the strong to help the weak, for those who have to share with those who have not.

It is true that this moral quality of man is often obscured, or even submerged, by other instincts. As we know too well, it does not prevent callous indifference to the fate of others or the brutal inhumanity of man to man. Nevertheless, it exists as a major incentive for men and women in the richer countries to assist the development of the less privileged ones. It would be a great mistake to underestimate this personal moral force.

Concern with the needs of other and poorer nations is

also the expression of a new and growing awareness that we belong to a world community, an awareness given a new impetus by our move into outer space.

The new experience of space may well be humanity's chief insight of the 1960s. Gradually entering the world's consciousness, like a silent and rising tide within the human imagination, are those pictures taken by earthmen from interstellar space showing our planet, full of light, hanging small, fragile and vulnerable, single and alone, in the cold void, with a oneness, a unity that suddenly takes on a new meaning.

As at least a quarter of the human race watched and waited together for the first man to step onto the moon, as children were wakened from sleep and peasants in far-off places crowded round village radio sets, as great crowds gathered in public squares, we may have witnessed the beginning of an irreversible modification of human consciousness.

In all truth, what was remote is now close; what was strange is now familiar. The man on the moon is real. There is, in a very literal sense, a new consciousness of the oneness of our world as we not only contemplate, but actually visit other planets.

Lopsided but unified, divided in resources and opportunities but united by knowledge and communications, the world of the 1960s takes into the next decade old divisions and disproportions, but also new challenges and opportunities—and, above all, this new concept of community and interdependence.

We now know that wars anywhere in the world can engage us all. The pollution of the environment in one place affects life everywhere. Epidemics and disease have no respect for national boundaries. Many of the challenges of development pose themselves in much the same way in the developed as in the developing countries. Our problems and our knowledge are universal, are planetary.

Every school child can now see more and know more of a land on the other side of the world than his great-grandfather may have seen or known of a city a hundred miles away. Young people, especially, know today that the population explosion, illiteracy and ignorance, poverty and pollution are global problems which threaten to make the world a torn and unhappy place. They are aware and acting members of the world, as well as of a national community. More than their elders—certainly more than their governments—they have a feeling of oneness in human development.

The drama of this moment in time lies in the fact that, on the one hand, we now have the knowledge and incentive to work toward a world community which recognizes the inescapability of interdependence, while, on the other, we do little enough to show such recognition in national, social, and economic policies. We cling to a world that is still composed of separate and competing sovereign states. We remain divided by the roots of our past when we should be searching for community based on the promise, or the menace, of our future.

It may seem unrealistic to the point of fantasy to talk of global community at a time when there is so much strife and discord in the world. If, by community, we meant absence of conflict, such talk would indeed be absurd, for in that sense of the word there would be very few national communities. It does make sense, however, to talk about, think about, and do what we can to encourage the concept of community which recognizes the compulsions of interdependence; which recognizes conflict and also the necessity, for very survival, of solving the problems that make for it.

Cooperation and aid for development is an important expression of this idea of community. It cannot, of course, eliminate violence and conflict, but it can help to create a common purpose which will at least make such elimination easier.

In today's world, concern with improvement of the human condition is no longer divisible. If the rich countries try to make it so, if they concentrate on poverty and backwardness at home and ignore it abroad, they will merely diminish and demean the principles by which they claim to live.

The acceleration of history, which is largely the result of the bewildering impact of modern technology, has changed the whole concept of national interest. Who can now ask where his country will be in a few decades without asking where the world will be? If we wish that world to be secure and prosperous, we must show a concern for the problems of *all* peoples. Individual citizens, in fact, often seem less confined than governments by the traditions of old-fashioned national policy and are more alive to the increasingly international character of human events and associations.

The rationality and the compulsions of this concept of community are major reasons for international cooperation for development. It is an assertion of faith in the future as well as conviction of the need to act now. It is a large part of the answer to the question, "Why aid?"

While the moral and the "community" case for cooperation for world development is valid and compelling, it is certainly not the full case. Indeed, it is not the sole, or to many not even the main, basis on which support should rest.

The Biblical parable of the Good Samaritan makes its own appeal, and it is a strong and unselfish one. But there is another parable which promises that if one casts his bread on the waters it will be returned a hundredfold. This also makes an appeal and provides an incentive of a different kind, that of national interest.

Self-interest that is enlightened and constructive is a sound and respectable basis for national policy. National advantage can legitimately be derived from international cooperation for the development of another country. The fullest possible utilization of all the world's resources, human and physical, which can be brought about by such cooperation helps not only those countries now economically weak, but also the strong and wealthy; it helps not only through direct benefits from a bilateral aid relationship, but also, and more importantly, through the general increase in trade which would follow general international development.

A growing and prosperous world economy, with all sharing in the growth, will be in everyone's interest and to everyone's advantage. Wretchedness and poverty in one part of the world, with the conflict and desperate hopelessness it creates, is bound to affect stability and progress in all other parts.

Foreign aid *is* a matter of national self-interest. Let there be no misunderstanding on that score. It is therefore of the highest importance to the developed countries not only that it should be adequate, but also that it should be effective.

It is also entirely reasonable that cooperation for development should result in a friendly political relationship on a basis of mutual respect. There is nothing to be criticized in that. We should be clear on two points, however.

First, an aid relationship should not be confused with a

political alliance, or designed for short-term political advantage, or merely to buy friends. An aid relationship is difficult in the best of circumstances. It becomes untenable if conditions requiring political support are attached to it.

Second, development will not normally create, nor should it be expected to create, immediate economic windfalls for a donor country.

It is, of course, tempting for governments to suggest, when they seek authority from their legislatures to transfer aid funds to other countries or to international agencies, that such a transfer will also mean direct national benefit of a commercial, political, or strategic character. It is a venerable tradition of diplomacy to see foreign policy and international relations in this light. But in the world of today it is inadequate and short-sighted; it ignores the broader concept of national self-interest which is essential in the new world.

That world, I repeat, is becoming—in spite of everything —a single, interdependent community, however difficult it may be at times to see this politically or economically. Moreover, this trend is irreversible since it is rooted in the scientific and technological revolution of our day.

We know now that our own national societies cannot possibly be stable and prosperous when privileged groups engross too much of the country's wealth, when conflict-making gaps between classes increase, when no acknowledged general interest controls and plans economic activity. All this we accept as self-evident within our country, but we are not yet ready to accept it for our world, even though, in that world, men and ideas can now move far more rapidly from Miami to Moscow than they could, a century ago, from London to Manchester.

Within our own countries, we no longer ask, "Why should

the rich people or rich regions be taxed more heavily to help underdeveloped areas?" National governments recognize such commitments as a firm priority obligation not only because it is morally repugnant to have one part of a national community live in affluence while others are poor and deprived, but also because they have learned that everyone benefits if the human and physical resources of a country are used to full capacity. The same concept is applicable to the world at large, and there should be a similar international commitment because the full use of the resources which remain undeveloped will, when developed, benefit both rich and poor nations.

*   *   *

Even when governments accept these international ideas in principle, they usually ignore them in practice and reject specific commitments arising out of them. Often they excuse their actions of evasion or rejection by complaining that it is impossible to do anything that would really benefit the poor countries. The problem, they say, is too vast and complex, it is beyond the reach of international cooperation. This is a defeatist view, but there is no doubt that the problem *is* vast and *is* complex. We have already seen that. Population in some countries is outstripping food production, though in others the situation has been reversed. There are mass migrations to cities, which are unprepared to receive them. There is growing unemployment, which may be on the order of 30 per cent in some areas of Latin America. The burden of misery in the poorer countries holds down markets and purchasing power and puts restraints on domestic growth, while the world market is filled with efficient Western competitors trying to maintain their historical advantage. Deadlocks seem to reinforce each other.

Not surprisingly, therefore, in some developing countries there is endemic violence, guerrilla insurrections, the robbing of banks, the kidnapping of ambassadors, tribal and sectional conflict, and even on occasion a disintegration of political order and social progress. It is perhaps not surprising that this turmoil brings about an attitude of impatience and negativism in some sections of opinion in developed countries, the kind of attitude that characterized so much respectable comment about the working classes and social change a century ago. They produce too many children. They don't work hard enough. They abuse the opportunities offered them. Give them coal and they put it in the bath tub. Give them a wage increase and they drink it up at the pub. Aid programs, in fact, are today often attacked for the same reasons that welfare payments were attacked fifty years ago, as wasteful and as an encouragement to loaf and procreate.

There is waste and stupidity and irresponsibility in every society, rich and poor, developed and developing. We only add to our own default, however, when we seek to justify it by exaggerating or imagining faults in others. There are more rational explanations than this for the falling off in the aid effort, and for the disenchantment that has spread in both developed and developing countries.

There has been disappointment over the inadequacy of the results already achieved and over the lack of appreciation for help given. This is in large part due to the fact that expectations were unrealistic. Too much was looked for too soon. The time-scale for achievement was misunderstood, and the resources required were underestimated by all concerned. Expectations of rapid "break-through" to self-sustaining growth ignored the century or more it has taken most modern economies to evolve. The new states had to learn that there is "no painless leap into modernity," that "instant" freedom doesn't mean "instant" progress. Failure to realize unrealistic and exaggerated hopes created later discouragement and disillusion.

Moreover, it was not always recognized that development, which often alters classes, occupations, and social structures, is normally disruptive, especially when resentment over past colonial dependence and the excitement of strident nationalism encourage and often provoke extremism.

These factors and circumstances help to explain, if not to justify, the weakening of the will to cooperate for development. George Woods, then President of the World Bank, put the situation in a few sentences in a speech to the Swedish Bankers' Association in Stockholm, October 27, 1967:

> The reason behind this slackening of effort is not only the normal pressure of domestic priorities on governments and peoples. It is also a belief that waste, inefficiency and even dishonesty have all too often deflected resources from development; to give more aid now, it is said, would simply send good money after bad. There are few Parliamentarians who do not have a favourite story of hair-raising waste. . . . Even some of the kinder critics question whether there is skill and administrative capacity enough in developing countries to absorb more capital, even if aid were to be increased. It is important therefore to try to disperse some of this gray fog of suspicion and discouragement by constant repetition of the actual facts.

It will be particularly difficult to "disperse" this "fog" for another category of critics—those who object to the whole idea of foreign aid, who argue that charity begins, and ends, at home unless it is a case of famine or some other natural disaster when, of course, all should behave as "good Christians" and help. "Aid," these critics claim, has weakened the will of some countries to help themselves by making them too dependent on outside help, most of which, in any event, was wasted. Therefore it is better for each nation to rely solely on itself: "each for itself, God for us all and the Devil take the hindmost," each making its own arrangements with its rich friends for assistance when necessary and attracting all the foreign capital it can for investment—and perhaps for later expropriation!

The idea that sovereign nations themselves might be part of a wider human community, which should cooperate in building up international ideas and institutions so that all men might survive and go forward together, is simply not part of the political horizon of such people. Foreigners are foreigners; "gooks" are "gooks." Beyond our frontiers lie those tribal enemies whom it has formerly been legitimate to defeat and, if necessary, to destroy; who can also be usefully exploited, but to whom we are bound by no nexus of neighborly obligation or political or social ties. From this feeling flow many of the criticisms of the irresponsibility and general misbehavior of other people. The bias with which such critics look at any economic assistance to foreigners leads them to seek first, and by instinct, evidence of corruption, waste, and inefficiency, and to ignore the fact that failures are often due to things as simple as a bad harvest or bad weather. We usually see what we want to see. If most of the human race is alien, and many are even enemies, then one can see the worst in them without much effort.

There are other critics who, while believing in international cooperation, have turned against foreign aid, as now practiced, because it is too closely linked to foreign policies or profit motivations of which they disapprove. They suspect that aid may be a cover for the domination of the poor and weak by the rich and strong, working through local privilege and power, a suspicion which is shared by many in the developing countries who are worried about what they call neocolonialism. This kind of objection goes even deeper. "Why," ask these critics, "should we transfer, or receive, under the guise of aid, the standards and manners of a society which makes man a cipher, a tool of impersonal corrupting forces over which he has no control and in the play of which he is lost?"

The more extreme among these critics even argue that if the present crisis in aid continues and deepens, this impasse is not to be deplored. It will encourage developing peoples to throw off their shackles, throw out their corrupt and reactionary governments, rid themselves of external influence and dependence. They could then enter into a genuine partnership for development in a more fraternal and peaceful world society, based on the rights and comradeship of all men.

*   *   *

So runs the argument against foreign aid—and, in running, overlooks some essential facts. To those who hold such views, however sincerely, about the principles and purposes of existing aid policies, especially those of the largest donors, I would concede the necessity for changes in the nature and organization of aid. But I would also emphasize that, within the present framework, capital resources transferred from outside and invested in agriculture *can* fend off starvation; invested in education these resources *can* produce lively, critical minds; used to help diversify and modernize an economy, they *can* break up old hierarchies of privilege. Indeed, the aid that is now denounced is already a major factor in producing, throughout the developing world, the sense of change, the feeling of new opportunity, without which entrenched traditions, whether they be feudal or racial or tribal or ideological, could continue unshaken for centuries.

So let us look at the reality: the reality of poverty, the reality of misery. This is where liberal internationalists and the generous young should be pointing. The vital question is: Can aid programs over the next two to three decades worsen or better the condition, social and economic, of these millions upon millions who at the moment lack so much that makes for a good human existence? If they can, they should be supported, even if the aid relationship is not perfect.

I have already mentioned, as another reason for opposition to aid, disappointment over results already achieved. I would like to return to this by examining the record. I believe that this record is a reason for continuing and strengthening development cooperation, not for opposing or abandoning it.

It will not be possible, however, to assess this record fairly unless we clearly realize that there are certain things that "aid" for economic development, or even development itself, cannot do, or should not be expected to do. Too often "aid" results are measured against impossible objectives.

- Aid itself cannot, in the first place, *guarantee* stable and self-sustaining development. It can only help.
- Aid, or even satisfactory economic development, how-

ever achieved, cannot ensure peace in the world or even within the developing countries themselves.

- Aid cannot ensure the success of representative democracy or of any other system of government.
- Aid cannot buy friends, or at least keep them bought.
- Economic development, even if made possible by massive transfers of Western resources, cannot itself bring about the "good life" for people, even though that life cannot exist in conditions of poverty, disease, and hunger.

It is in the light of these cautionary observations that the record of aid and cooperation for economic development should be examined.

Naturally, that record shows mistakes and failures. Some of them have been spectacular and have, of course, been sensationally publicized. Failure or folly is always good for a big headline, while quiet and steady achievement usually has no reporter to sing its praises. Naturally, also, the mistakes and the failures have been exaggerated and exploited by those who are opposed in principle, and in politics, to foreign aid.

There is no doubt that in earlier years many things went wrong. There was much to be learned, both on the donor and receiving sides, in order to make cooperation for development effective. After all, such cooperation was something unprecedented in history. There was bound to be much trial and some error.

Transfers of resources were often more closely related to a strategy of cold war than to a strategy for development. Some customs and procedures that operated against effective use of aid could not be changed quickly and some resisted any change. There was wastage, even if not more than might have been expected in the circumstances that existed and had existed in receiving countries for centuries.

The captious and superior attitude usually adopted by critics ignored these circumstances, as it often ignored the fact that this kind of wastage occurs from time to time in their own domestic program. *Any* wastage, of course, is to be deplored, especially in countries not rich enough to afford it; but, in relation to the size and complexity of the resource transfers involved and to other circumstances, the losses from wastage do not appear to have been excessive.

A more important loss, which is not usually thought of as wastage, came from the allocation of aid to programs and projects that had little to do with development or, at least, should have been further down in the priority list as being more concerned with prestige and politics than with economic growth.

Here again, the fault, like the pressure, was not all on one side. As the years went on, however, the situation improved. Experience has led to better results as measured by genuine development. The organization and administration of financial and economic policies in receiving countries have also improved and so have the planning and allocation procedures of donors. This improvement is a major reason why it would be especially tragic if development cooperation were abandoned or weakened at the very time when it is becoming more effective in securing the objectives laid down.

We should not forget that a strong and sustained development effort in Asia and Africa is hardly more than twenty years old. You do not blame a child for not winning an open hundred-yard dash. What you should worry about is whether its legs are growing straight and strong and whether the child is moving faster and more steadily. If that is the case, then you can say that the child is doing well. On this score, most of the developing countries are doing well. But we must always keep in mind the length of the time-span required for people to be drawn out of their old static habits, to be taught and to apply new methods of production to agriculture and industry, to cope with all the complex problems of a new urban order. These inescapable problems of modernization, as we are learning, take time to solve, even in richer and economically advanced industrial societies.

Therefore, we should appreciate why, in the short period that international cooperation for the development of poorer countries has been going on, nothing like self-sustaining development could have been achieved. Even the most successful of all the development programs that the modern world has seen took fifty years. This was the transformation of Japan after the Meiji revolution between 1870 and 1914, during which the whole framework and basis of a modern economy was laid. The transformation of Britain and America took longer, and in more propitious circumstances. Why, then, should we expect new, developing countries in a short period of time to achieve results that must, by definition, lie in the future?

Our Commission on International Development spent a year looking as carefully as we could into the development record of this short period of twenty years. We were unanimous in our conclusion that encouraging progress has been made in developing countries and that the ground is now well laid for further advances in the future.

The record shows that the cooperative development effort of the last twenty years has been, by any historical comparison, unprecedented. Never before in history has there been such a huge voluntary transfer of resources from one group of states to another. Moreover, those who said that the new, developing nations would lack the administrative efficiency and the political experience to use any of this assistance effectively, have been proven wrong. Not only has the average growth rate of the newly independent developing countries during this period been much higher than during their colonial period; it has also been higher than the average of any comparable period in the nineteenth century among the rich, industrialized countries of today. It now appears that the United Nations development target of 5 per cent per year for the decade of the 1960s will be met, despite the fact that the expected aid, based on an accepted figure of 1 per cent of GNP, has not been received.

There has, of course, been a great diversity in performance. Twenty-three countries achieved an average growth rate of over 5 per cent in the 1960s, but there were at least twenty-four countries—including some of the largest and poorest—whose growth rate in this period was less than 4 per cent.

If we take income per head, the record is not so good, though still historically impressive. Some forty-one developing countries have, since 1955, managed average growth in income per capita of 2 per cent or more for a ten-year period. This is roughly what the developed countries of Western Europe and North America achieved in the hundred years after 1850.

The savings rate from 1960 to 1967 was on the average about 22 per cent. This is very important, for it means that, as the economy goes on growing, the scale of savings will grow too, with all that this means for development.

The total result, then, has been encouraging, but it is not

adequate to enable the countries concerned to achieve by themselves sustaining growth in a reasonable time. In spite of the over-all progress made, the impact from economic development on the poverty of individuals comprising nearly two-thirds of the world's population is still pitifully small. Living conditions in most developing areas remain well below the standard of Europe before the industrial revolution. Well over half of the people of developing countries still must survive on average annual money incomes below $100 a year. With the rapid rise in population, the improvement in income per head is often imperceptible—a couple of dollars a year.

Moreover, progress in development has often been much more satisfactory than the distribution of its benefits. People live longer, but in many cases no better. Many more children are in school, but the education they are receiving is often irrelevant to their own and their country's real needs. There remain, as we have seen, immense problems of uncontrolled urban migration and unemployment. Even the encouraging, indeed, exciting results of the "Green Revolution" in agriculture have created new problems as well as removed old ones.

So, while we can reject categorically the argument that the record of the past twenty years justifies the weakening, let alone the abandonment, of the aid and development effort, we have no right to be complacent over the results already achieved.

The main responsibility, as I have already said, for accelerating and enlarging these achievements rests, and must continue to rest, with the developing countries themselves. Nothing of lasting importance can be accomplished except through their own efforts. Aid is no fairy godmother touching everything with her magic wand so that, presto, the little mice and pumpkins of local effort are turned into large luxury carriages. Development is a long, slogging, grinding effort by the people themselves of each country. If they don't make that effort, there will be no development.

Up to the present, external aid has probably not accounted for more than a fraction of the results from national effort. This fraction, however, can be of critical importance in removing or minimizing external constraints on developing countries, providing greater policy flexibility for them, widening the range of options open to them and thereby increasing, not decreasing, their independence and self-reliance.

Even the most resolute national effort for growth is likely, in present conditions, to be frustrated by shortages of capital, of foreign exchange, of technical assistance and know-how. The developing countries cannot quickly escape from their need for these things; without them, their own resources often cannot be mobilized. This is where foreign aid comes in.

To be sure, there is a danger that such aid might blunt the will to self-help when it is the wrong kind of aid, or given or taken for the wrong reasons. For example, food aid has encouraged some countries to neglect changes in agricultural policy for too long. But aid for genuine economic development not only helps ease critical shortages, but should help to build a firm base for independent and self-reliant growth. Until that base is built, most developing countries will be faced with acute problems of dependence on factors outside their borders. From this dependence, we should never forget, they are even more anxious to escape than we are to have them do so. Evidence of this is to be found in the fact that, poor as they are, the domestic savings of the developing countries in the 1960s financed 85 per cent of their total investment, considerably more on the average than was the case with the developed countries during the last century when many conditions were far more advantageous for development.

It is the very fact that these countries are living at the margin that makes the contribution of external aid, though marginal, so important. It can mean the difference between staying comfortably ahead of population growth, while steadily increasing public services and welfare, and barely keeping pace with that growth, thereby not going forward economically at all. A difference of 20 per cent in imports—and, on the average, foreign assistance has financed 20 per cent of imports from the industrialized countries—can mean the difference between growth and stagnation for a developing country.

Finally, I want to say a word about the Treasury argument against "aid": that we can't afford it; that the "burden of aid" is too heavy for the hard-pressed taxpayers of the rich countries. Let us look at the facts:

- In 1968, total aid transfers from all countries were valued at $12,753,000,000. Of this, total official transfers, which alone constitute a burden on the taxpayer, amounted, at the most generous calculation, to $6.4 billion, which was $200 million less than the previous year.
- This figure for official "aid" may seem large, but, as a percentage of the total GNP, it was 0.39 per cent. Seven years previously, in 1961, it was 0.54 per cent.
- Reverse flows, such as interest payments on loans, ex-

port credits, profits taken out, and capital imports from the developing countries, reduced aid figures substantially; some say by more than $2 billion in 1968.

- Also, in many cases, practically all of this "aid" is tied to the purchase of goods and services in the donor country, which brings substantial returns to that country, though it may reduce the value of the aid to the recipient country by as much as 20 per cent.

- Aid has also been used for defense support and to dispose of surpluses, notably agricultural surpluses in supporting the agricultural subsidy policies of a donor country.

- The "burden"—even if you take the highest figure— represents about $6 for every person in the wealthy industrialized countries. This would not appear to be excessive for countries which supported an arms burden of $140 billion in 1968 and whose gross national product increased during that same year by $130 billion.

- The Commission on International Development has recommended that, within the total figure of 1 per cent of GNP for all transfers, official aid should reach, by 1975, 0.7 per cent of GNP. If present growth rates are projected over that period, this would mean an increase of $9.5 billion in official aid over five years, again excluding the compensating reverse figures I have mentioned.

- It has been estimated that by 1975 the developed countries will have increased their total GNP by $600 billion to $650 billion, if we accept a modest projection of 3 per cent annual growth rate and do not alter present tax rates. Of this increase in GNP, less than 1.5 per cent would go to aid under the 0.7 per cent formula.

Clearly, within such a pattern of growth, the "burden of aid" is not excessive.

Surely there can be no valid argument that an aid effort of this magnitude is too heavy to be borne. I know that there are inflationary and other pressures now beating against developed economies. So the question is asked: If we add to official domestic expenditures even these relatively small amounts for "aid," will they not dangerously increase economic strains and inflationary risks? Might not further demands on the Treasury do so much harm to our own economies that the consequent failure to grow might mean only a higher percentage of a lower total for developing countries, with a net loss for them?

Economic pressure and spending priorities are, of course, very subjective things. At the height of the postwar crisis, when the whole future of Europe seemed in doubt and when, to help secure it, the Marshall Plan was launched by a generous, confident United States, something like 2 per cent of the gross national product was involved in the transfer of capital from the United States across the Atlantic. That brilliantly successful program was of essential importance in the rebuilding of Europe, with the consequences that we know. But in 1947, no one could have forecast this good result. And the people of America were under greater economic pressures then than now, with a national income not even half of what it is today.

If 2 per cent of gross national product could be afforded in 1948, after the financial effort and strain of a world war, 0.7 per cent for official aid can surely be afforded now after more than twenty years of increasing prosperity.

But, of course, the question for the United States, and for every other developed country—for all should accept the same obligation—is not one of economic fact, but of political will; of what our spending priorities should be in changing domestic circumstances and mounting domestic pressures. Here the situation is less clear. Our wants grow with our incomes. We can feel poor at $10,000 a year, poor at $20,000 a year, even poor at $50,000 a year. The pressure we feel at all these levels of income is not in any sense an objective or calculable thing. When the urge to reduce public expenditure is strong and the demands for new services are great, foreign economic assistance has to compete with many other pressing needs. This we have to recognize. But we must also try to keep a sense of proportion in our assessment of pressures and priorities.

The expenditure on arms by developed countries, as I have said, is now around $140 billion a year. A very small cutback in these terrific—and terrifying—arms expenditures could be used for cooperation in the peaceful work of development and thereby give not less, but more, security, as well as many other benefits.

How can one accept an arms-spending of $140 billion a year, which cannot give security on any enduring basis, and argue at the same time that $6.4 billion, less than one-half of 1 per cent of a GNP which had increased during the year by at least $130 billion, spent on official transfers for development aid (a substantial part of which we get back) is not economically bearable?

The question, then, is not one of capacity, but will; not whether we can afford to spend this money on development aid, but whether we can afford *not* to spend it.

III

The Politics of the Problem

In the previous lecture I tried to show that "aid" at the level of 1 per cent of gross national product is easily bearable by the developed countries; that the problem was one of will, not of economics. This makes it, above all, a problem of politics.

Indeed, problems of international aid and development co-operation are bound to be more political, in the broad sense of that word, than economic. Nor will we make much headway in dealing with these problems unless we understand the politico-economic relationship. This means, among other things, appreciating the sensitivities, the prides and even the prejudices, of the governments and peoples of developing countries. It also means, however, that those countries in their turn should understand the limitations on policy and action in the normal operation of democratic government in developed countries.

Misunderstanding, which leads to later difficulty and trouble, can also arise from the discovery that, even with foreign aid, instant development does not automatically follow the achievement of freedom, that it takes time to build up the institutions and the techniques of growth.

Local people must be trained and educated. A country's present and potential resources must be surveyed so that the investments made will prove productive. There must be willingness to allocate resources in sensible proportions between consumption and savings. Increased consumer goods are what the people will want, and they are likely to judge their governments by the success in supplying them. The wise leader, however, will disregard the immediate political popularity that may come from a generous consumer policy in order to invest in future economic growth. Unfortunately, there is always the danger that, if he does, he may soon cease to be in a position to lead at all!

It is natural, where brief experience has not yet produced full understanding, that there should be insistent and, at times, unreasonable requests for foreign aid in the hope that it will help to perform miracles of economic growth. It is also to be expected that on occasion aid will help to maintain a government in power as well as make life better for people.

There has been growth, but no miracles. Indeed, the development gap between the rich and poor nations is not narrowing, but widening, and political consequences, in the long run, can be as important as the economic.

The widening of the gap between rich and poor may not result in the menace of nuclear war that comes from the political division of the world between two superpowers with conflicting policies and ideologies, with fear and hostility between them. Nevertheless, the problems inherent in the material gap are explosive and incalculable, and there will be neither security nor stability in the world if they are not solved. The situation is doubly dangerous when it is exploited in a cold war by one side or the other, when the issues involved in development cooperation become more strategic than economic.

There is another political problem. Economic development in many parts of the world becomes mixed up with the transition of peoples from colonialism to independence. This transition and the problems it brings arouse a host of emotions and neuroses that go with a nationalism that has been long suppressed by rulers of another race and color and then suddenly, and usually without sufficient preparation, achieves sovereign independence.

The resulting pressures on the new leaders and governments are made more insistent by the circumstances of their accession to power, by hopes of immediate prosperity for all, now that freedom has been won. Then later, in the cold gray dawn after the night of celebration, the new rulers learn that political stability and economic progress is achieved, not by banners and parades, but only by work and sacrifice; not merely by expelling others, but by disciplining one's self.

Some leaders may shrink from facing up, or asking their people to face up, to hard reality. They may try to divert the populace and save themselves by circuses at home and adventures abroad. When we are critical about lapses of this kind, we should remember that they occur also, and with less excuse, in older and more stable societies.

Similarly when we complain of inefficiency in the administration of aid, of disappointing and inadequate results from cooperation, we should realize that development in the newly independent countries involves problems that are wider and more complex than economic growth alone.

It is to the credit of the new countries that, for the most part, they have not dissolved in chaos and have faced up responsibly to their problems. In some cases, however, the pressures have been too much for them; order and authority have given way to extremism, of right or left, and even at times to anarchy.

When this happens, cooperation for development becomes difficult, often impossible. It will be tempting, however unjustified, for national leaders to throw the blame on external causes. This will be the easier because of the envy, and even hostility, that poorer nations normally feel toward the rich. The feeling, as we know, usually has a historical and political foundation. It is not sufficiently explained by hunger and poverty and will not be dispelled merely by filling bellies and dental cavities. Failure to understand this is often due to the persistent fallacy that developing peoples, whom we still too often think of as the backward heathen of our Sunday School classes, were really happier when they lived in a state of natural and undeveloped innocence—and ignorance; that they really want no part of our industrial progress. They may not want—and I have already said that I hope they will not get—the kind of development which will result in neon-nightmares, high-rise cave dwellings, and psychiatric clinics. But they do want to be able to stand up in dignity, decency, and self-respect, as well as to eat more, be sick less, and live longer. Development is for them not an economic option so much as a political necessity. It is part of their unfinished revolution and, somehow, with or without our help, they are determined to achieve it.

In any event, it is quite irrelevant to speculate on whether they were better off in their earlier state, which was, perhaps, tolerable for them if only because they knew nothing else. Now most of them do know something else. We may not know *them* very well, but they know *us*. (We ourselves have made that possible by our technological progress in com-

munications.) They also know that now no man's lot is or-
dained or inevitable, that they can live not only longer, but
better. Even if the masses are only partially aware of all this,
their leaders and governments know it, in detail and by
dialogue, and these are the people with whom the developed
world must deal.

So there is not much point in protesting, as some people
do, that the masses in the poor and developing countries are
not really interested in freedom and politics, that they would
have been content to live as they have lived for centuries if
only leaders with Oxford or Harvard or Columbia degrees
had left them alone and had not used them as stepping
stones to their own political and personal goals. This is not
true. The emerging, awakened peoples are emphatically not
content to remain poor and passive in a changing world.
They are no longer impressed by what the rich, white,
Western countries may have done in the past and are still
doing to help improve the lot of the deprived and poor non-
whites. Dr. Schweitzer is not enough. They are no longer
willing merely to sit back and rely on the United Nations or
on a benevolent foreign government to build hospitals for
them and improve their agriculture. Freedom has now stimulated them to move forward on their own. The racial
inequality and discriminations they have suffered in the past
have spurred on the movement. Nationalism has put pride
behind it.

We must accept the fact that this nationalism, with its
attitude to development, is often possessed of a genuine sense
of both economic and political grievance, the background of
which I have already mentioned, and is often nourished in
the conviction that it has been the victim of repression, social, political, and economic. The feeling is moderating in

THE POLITICS OF THE PROBLEM 59

most of the new developing countries, while in a few it was never extreme. But it cannot be ignored if development co-operation is to be politically, as well as economically, constructive.

A regrettable aspect of this sense of grievance, where it still exists, is that it may take the eyes of national leaders off the real problems of development. History shows that all colonial revolutionaries in the period of pre-independence planning and preparation tend to explain their country's deprivations in a simple formula of exploitation. Everything from a miscarriage of justice to a bad harvest is blamed on the "imperialists" who hold power against the "will of the people." The struggle for freedom and the fervor of the ideals it inspires create a belief that the transfer of power will, of itself, work wonders. Then, when wonders are not worked, it is tempting to make the former imperial power the scapegoat on whom all failures and evils are blamed. If progress after independence is not considered to be satisfactory, the leaders can go on for years explaining away their failure as due to their legacy of imperialism. They can use their former rulers as bogeys to explain away poverty and distress. This, of course, may have some historical basis of reason, but it may also hinder the forthright effort required to grapple with the real and existing causes of poverty and backwardness. And it makes international cooperation for development more difficult.

It is not only in the developing countries that attitudes may be conditioned by a consciousness of earlier exploitation. Many Westerners, especially in former imperial countries, who are more sensitive or sympathetic than most of their fellows, nourish a sense of guilt in their relationship with the hungry and impoverished of Africa and Asia. They may accept, not always even consciously, the reproach that backward peoples are backward merely because they have been abused and oppressed and that the rich man's sin—exploitation—can be expiated by a transfer of resources until the "victims" have reached something approaching our standard of living. We can ease our conscience by helping them "live better electrically." Such people are usually generous-hearted and good and wish to act in the Christian tradition. Their feeling, based on a sense of moral responsibility, is one of the strongest and best incentives for assistance to developing countries, as I have already pointed out. It is wiser, however, to approach the problem of aid for development not so much as an opportunity for expiation as one for cooperation to mutual advantage; as neither restitution nor charity, but as wise national policy involving a national commitment, which should be accepted and whose discharge must be given a high priority. How can this commitment be best discharged?

*   *   *

A single, satisfactory formula or strategy covering every aspect of development cooperation is not possible; conditions vary too much. Yet there are certain principles that should govern the aid relationship between all developed and developing countries. Arrangements which contradict these basic and essential principles will prejudice the whole international effort. Indeed, these principles rest on a common political and even philosophical approach to cooperation in this field.

The first of these principles is partnership, based on mutual interest and mutual understanding. It must be made a reality that will cover all sectors of an integrated development front, in the full breadth and depth of its meaning, joining donor and recipient in a finite enterprise which will benefit both. It should not be determined by the vagaries of the current political climate, domestic or international. Nor should aid be extended or withheld in accordance with that climate.

Such a partnership concept would replace the narrower, too one-sided donor-receiver relationship with the idea of cooperation for orderly and progressive world development in whose benefits all would share.

This was the philosophy which underlay the Report of the Commission on International Development. The Report seeks to give an over-all view of the operations, organization, and importance of international cooperation for development and to provide a rationale for such international cooperation. It makes proposals for a general over-all strategy that is fitted into the general framework of the international economy and takes into consideration the circumstances of different countries and areas. It integrates proposals, hitherto advocated in isolation, into such a general strategy, with indications how they may be specifically implemented. It offers a balanced picture of the respective responsibilities of the developing and the developed countries in an effective and constructive partnership. It brings out the significant progress which the developing countries have already achieved and the lessons which have been learned, which show that although underdevelopment is an evil, man now has the power to eradicate it.

In the eradication of this evil, in reducing the material gap between the two worlds, the quantity of aid is not the only consideration. Quality and utilization are equally important. There is no point in making vast sums available if they cannot be used wisely; if there are not the engineers, the technicians, the teachers or the administrators to make projects work; if the essential exploratory work of survey, analysis, and preparation has not been done.

As a result, a project or a program may sometimes be held up while planning and surveys go on. But it may also mean that waste has been avoided and, what is even more important, that energies and resources will not be diverted into projects, the collapse of which in a few years' time would weaken the foundations of a new country and prejudice the possibility of further aid. We must try to avoid this kind of failure, which not only disillusions the receiving country but naturally has a sour effect on the taxpayers of the countries that provide funds for aid.

It may be understandable, but it is naive and unrealistic, to press for the immediate allocation of large sums for foreign aid in the hope that the flow itself will bring quick, easy, and rewarding results. This is too simple. Far more than mere financial transfers are required.

Aid is a long-term problem of vast complexity and many ramifications. It is not merely one of finding more dollars, or even more experts. It is one of cooperation, organization, and understanding on a broad international front.

It will not be solved merely by transferring Western money or Western values or Western ideas and techniques to societies where they may not work—or should not be expected to.

For instance, if industrial growth in new countries is to be soundly based and become self-sustaining, this cannot be achieved simply by introducing Western equipment, production, and marketing techniques. There will have to be a flexible approach which makes allowance for local conditions.

The industrial productivity of the West is supported by a wide-ranging modern economy. Capital and skilled services of all kinds are available. Machines can be acquired readily at reasonable cost. In the underdeveloped countries, all this may be lacking. Substitutes must be created for supporting services and often for modern technical equipment. In these countries with their oversupply of labor and an undersupply of capital and equipment, industries cannot, in the economist's language, be as "capital-intensive" as they are in more highly developed countries of the West. Aid, therefore, should be adapted to the conditions of the country where it is to be used. The "know-how" that works in Kenosha may not be successful without modification in Kandy. Similarly, while development requires the raising of educational standards, this does not necessarily mean basing them on the ideas and methods that have been acceptable in the past in Europe and North America, where, incidentally, they do not seem to be so generally acceptable now.

Technical assistance means building up the basic infrastructure for progress, helping to expand and modernize industry and, even more important, agriculture. It means educational and research training abroad for students from developing countries; and even more—because too many of them stay abroad—it means building at home the institutions of training and research as well as of general education suited to the conditions of the developing countries and regions.

What is needed is imagination on the part of businessmen and economists, planners and technicians, in adapting Western experience to very different conditions. Too great complacency over the superiority of Western methods can unfortunately produce a rigidity of mind in the face of novel

challenges, a stubborn refusal to adapt to different requirements, and an impatience with the customs of other peoples,
which seem to Westerners to stand in the way of a productive collaboration for industrial development. This problem
is complicated by the fact that Western economic progress
is based not only on its technology but also on its own customs and manners. The kind of interpersonal relationships,
however, which produce the required incentives and techniques for the successful working of our Western industrial
and economic system do not necessarily obtain in nations
with very different social and cultural patterns.

If industrial and other forms of development cooperation
are to be effective and successful, local factors must be taken
into consideration. I do not mean that progress may not
require change. It *will,* as is increasingly, even impatiently,
recognized by the developing countries themselves. In some
cases, indeed, development may be impossible if certain local
traditions, habits of social exploitation, and inertia are not
altered. Such change, however, can best be made by altera-
tions and adaptations that are guided by local leaders rather
than by swift disruption resulting from an effort at sudden
revolutionary conversion to Western methods. In our assistance programs, therefore, we need engineers, scientists and
businessmen, who are also psychologists, sociologists and
even anthropologists. This suggestion doesn't mean that they
should all have Ph.D.s before they are sent to serve abroad.
All that is required—but it is much—is the kind of understanding and integrity which has in the past distinguished so
many of our missionaries, doctors, and teachers *"in partibus
infidelibus."*

Even with a perceptive and sensitive concern for local
conditions, it will not be possible to avoid all difficulties in

an aid relationship with the newly independent countries of Asia and Africa, or with the older independent countries of Latin America. It will help to reduce and resolve these difficulties, however, if we remember that, in these countries as in our own, considerations other than those of economic growth are often important, and occasionally overriding. Moreover, political or social considerations that often seem to get in the way of economic progress may at times have their own validity. Even when they seem irrational from outside, it may be dangerous and unwise to dismiss them as such. Developing governments may be foolish to give a high priority to steel mills more for prestige than for economic purposes, or to produce things with which the world is oversupplied merely because they have been producing them for generations and because their social and economic systems have been built around such production. We have to be careful, however, in linking our advice and our aid to the sudden abandonment of both old practices and new prides. Nevertheless, we can try to show that the price poorer countries may be paying for certain customs and practices is far too high in economic terms, that insistence on paying it will prevent development, and that our cooperation with that kind of policy just will not be effective and, therefore, for a long time, not possible.

There are good economic reasons why some of these nations that are very small should not even try to exist as independent and viable economic units at all. But don't expect these reasons to impress the government and citizens of a new state, however small. New countries may also learn in due course that they can develop and prosper only by outward-looking and liberalized economic policies, or by forming regional associations with other countries. But this is something they will have to find out for themselves, with the persuasion and help we can give them by example even more than by precept.

*   *   *

Another problem, which I have already mentioned, often has to be faced in cooperation for development because it has an important bearing on the aid relationship. Should there be conditions or "strings" attached to economic aid? What is the proper relationship between a government providing assistance and the regime in power in the recipient country? Should aid be given to a country if it strengthens the hands of a corrupt and reactionary government? To what extent should aid be used to promote needed reform?

These are questions for which there are no simple or dogmatic answers. With the aid from smaller developed countries, like Canada, the problem is not too acute. Such aid is, in most cases, relatively small in the aggregate, and is not likely to have any substantial political impact. But the "aid" policy of the United States, the United Kingdom, or France could make or break a local regime in a small and poor country, and indeed has done so.

The policies of the major Western powers have not always been above reproach in using aid for a political purpose. In too many cases they have supported, by economic as well as by other forms of aid, regimes which stood in the way of necessary social and economic reform but which had acquired a merit badge by professing themselves to be vigorously anti-Communist or pro-Western and strong supporters of the donor country. At times, indeed, anti-Communism, and political support for it, has been used as the main argument for aid.

Aid, even when extended solely for legitimate purposes of economic development and without any political motive, can serve to strengthen politically a government in power. In doing so, it may postpone domestic reforms that are necessary to set an economy on the upward spiral and bring about greater social progress as well. For Washington, London, or Paris, however, the alternatives are not easy. They are damned if they interfere and damned if they don't. If the situation is bad enough, they may feel they should put strong pressure on an existing regime through withholding any kind of aid, in order to bring about conditions which will justify that aid. But this involves at least negative intervention, and intervention is denounced as a cardinal sin in every international organization from the United Nations to the Organization of American States. The fact that it may be intervention in a good cause is not sufficient justification to many because the question inevitably arises as to who is the judge of its goodness. There may be occasions when there is no alternative to cutting off aid, which may, it is hoped, result in "throwing the rascals out," though not invariably. But the implications of any such action, its effect on people as opposed to their governments, should be fully considered by those who lightly demand that the donor countries refuse to give development assistance to any regime which it considers to be totalitarian and extremist, either on the Right or the Left.

The fact is that at times development assistance will be justified, however much the regime or system of government is to be deplored. Let me cite a few examples. In a developing country, the condition of agriculture will often determine whether people can be fed from their own soil. Hybrids are facts. Fertilizer is a fact. Better water supplies are facts. Irrigation is a fact and may be the key to life in China or in India. River control may be the key to irrigation. Foreign aid may be required for all these things and for very practical reasons.

We cannot, in short, maintain that politics alone should determine aid policies if we are concerned with helping people. Surely the best way is to select those projects and programs for development aid which are least likely to have the wrong political impact and most likely to be beneficial to all the people of the country concerned, disregarding the form of government as long as that government and its leaders have shown by their actions that they are committed to economic growth which is to the benefit of all the people in the country.

I know that this is not as simple as it may sound. It is against our democratic grain to transfer anything to a dictator, even if it will be of help to his people who need it.

Also, when a government in power, "respectable" in our terms, wants economic aid for a particular purpose or project, the value of which seems very doubtful, it is not easy for foreign or international agencies to insist on aid for something else. Arguments for an alternative program or project that will make for sounder development and benefit more people may be strong in theory but may come up against vested interests, local customs, nationalist feeling, and many other forces over which economic reason does not easily prevail but which may not be as harmful in themselves as we think. The recipient government may turn out to be right in the position it takes. What looks like wise aid policy in the council chambers of Washington or London may often be too doctrinaire for the realities of a situation in Africa or Asia.

In short, there is no formula which really solves all the problems, economic, political, and even psychological, which arise out of something so complicated and difficult as an aid relationship. Undoubtedly, "strings" are bad if they tie you to the wrong things, or tie up the wrong kind of parcel. It is true, for instance, that in the earlier stages of the cold war there may have been too strong a tendency in the United States to associate economic assistance with military collaboration and to look upon "neutralism" as incompatible with such assistance. But, in recent years, there has been an increasing understanding that a neutralist or uncommitted attitude makes a good deal of sense for a new and weak country and should not prejudice agreement on aid programs.

In other words, political or economic strings can be crude and tight, in which case they probably defeat their own purpose. But they can also be reasonable and loose. In either case, the country that needs aid is constantly aware of a very real "string" in the fact that the continuation of that aid, if it is bilateral, is at the pleasure of the donor country; that the taxpayers and legislators of that country, even though they may be generous and patient, are not likely to assist a recipient which is consistently and actively hostile and malevolent to them. Nor should the donors be expected to do so, or to give any special help to a country which gives direct aid and comfort to their declared and active enemies. Likewise, while an enlightened donor country should have no desire, as it has no right, to insist on privileges for the private investment of its own citizens in a foreign state in return for official economic aid, yet the receiving country must realize that reasonable respect is necessary for the legitimate rights of those investors and that they should not be treated unfairly and discriminated against if legislators are to remain well disposed.

There is one form of "strings" which recipients of aid specifically object to, known as "tying." It is an arrangement which provides that the capital being allocated for aid should be spent in the donor country and, at times, for a particular product. This, of course, may be a limitation on the quantity and quality of the aid available, within the amount allocated. Indeed, tying can reduce the value of aid received by as much as 20 per cent. It can also alter priorities in recipient countries, create administrative complications, as well as interfere with the growth of trade, especially among the developing countries.

Tying also has some harmful effects on the donors. Foreign trade patterns are distorted, and inefficient industries are overprotected.

Tying is often explained to be necessary because of the balance-of-payments problems faced by several countries. It is to be hoped that the recent agreement by the International Monetary Fund to create Special Drawing Rights, "paper gold," may help to lessen these problems and provide an opportunity for a collective attack on the "tying" problem, which is the only way it can be successfully dealt with.

The Report of the Commission on International Development recommends certain specific steps that should be taken in order to make some progress toward untying aid. (1) Aid-givers should undertake not to intensify their tying procedures; (2) a study of the principal balance-of-payments losses and gains likely to arise from untying should immediately be commissioned by the Development Assistance Committee of OECD in cooperation with the International Monetary Fund for report by the middle of 1970; and (3) on the basis of this report, a conference of major donors should be called to consider the progressive untying of bilateral and multilateral aid.* It is to be hoped that these steps can be taken.

*   *   *

This brings me to a related subject, also with political implications: How should aid transfers be allocated and administered?

It has been argued that the suspicion and misunderstanding that is at times created or brought to the surface by foreign "aid" could be exorcised or reduced if aid arrangements between two countries could be replaced by aid allocated and organized by international agencies. The former, bilateral aid, is often considered to be too closely tied to the foreign policy interests of the donor power or to be a form of national charity. This will create, inevitably, the suspicions and misunderstandings I have mentioned, especially if the aid comes from a big power. As Senator Fulbright put it, discussing American aid:

> In its present bilateral form foreign aid, though composed principally of interest-bearing loans, is run as a kind of charity, demeaning to both recipient and donor. In addition, it is becoming a vehicle for deep American involvement in areas and issues which lie beyond both our vital interests and our competence.

Therefore, it is held, responsibility for the planning and allocation of aid should be shifted from national governments, against which there may be built-in suspicions and prejudices, to the international community as a whole and

* *Partners in Development* (New York: Praeger Publishers, 1969), pp. 174–75.

distributed through international organizations, which, representing all, might be considered objective by all. In Senator Fulbright's words: "The rich pay not as a private act of *noblesse oblige* but in fulfillment of a social responsibility; the poor receive benefits not as a lucky gratuity but as the right of citizens."*

This argument is also supported by people who are dismayed by the confusion of national agencies engaged in aid-giving and want to tidy things up by turning over all activities in this field to one or two international institutions. The thesis is an attractive one and has merit, but, if it is carried too far, it will be found to be neither practicable nor desirable. There is so much variety in the field of development cooperation, so much need for pragmatism and for *ad hoc* judgments, so many separate political and economic factors to be considered on both sides, that any procedure or policy, however sensible in theory, which presumes to cover the whole world situation and operate through one or two international agencies, is not likely to be successful in practice.

Furthermore, international bodies are also political, and political forces, often intense ones, operate within them. The United Nations itself cannot be looked upon as something completely detached, orbiting in an outer space of impartiality. Even if the Secretariat and its experts responsible for the administration of aid programs are considered as impersonal and denationalized, working without national fear or favor, they are international public servants subject to direction by the governmental representatives on United Nations bodies in which political conflicts and rivalries operate. Anyone with any experience of the United Nations knows of the

* J. William Fulbright, *The Arrogance of Power* (New York: Random House, 1967), pp. 223–24.

play of these political forces, the maneuvering of blocs, the continuous tug-of-war between and among developed and developing countries.

When I speak in these terms of the United Nations as a political body, I do not do so to criticize or disparage it. It must be that kind of institution in the world in which it has to operate. Conflicting political forces must be taken into consideration and, in the effort to reconcile these forces and various pressure groups, there is always the risk of distorting the purposes and the effectiveness even of aid programs.

We should not assume, therefore, that there would be no political pressures or difficulties in working through international agencies. The developing countries now play an increasingly important role in the United Nations. They have a decisive number of votes. They look to the world organization as an arm of their foreign policies more than do the great powers. They are also quick to detect in United Nations policy anything that seems to them to be dictated by the interests of the rich Western members, even when it is cloaked in deceptively idealistic resolutions. Some of their persisting attitudes to the United Nations were formed in the days when Western power was dominant in the organization. That day is over, but the memory lingers on.

My reservations notwithstanding, I believe in increasing aid through multilateral channels. There are many things which are better done multilaterally with less likelihood of arousing suspicions or creating political pressures than if the aid came from a powerful Western country. While it may be an illusion to believe that we could wisely put all our funds for aid into one great pool, administered on entirely scientific principles by the United Nations, the World Bank, or some new organization for world development, international agencies should be used to a greater extent than at present, especially to promote a more rational distribution of aid and the establishment of acceptable criteria for allocation and for objective monitoring of performance. Since such agencies do have a world-wide responsibility and can look at the whole picture, they can see where there is duplication or contradiction or omission and can point out failure to discharge commitments undertaken.

Within this universal framework, however, room must be left for national and regional programs to be carried out through bilateral or regional arrangements. It is idle to imagine that the donors—especially the major ones—will at present agree to surrender all, or even most of, their bilateral aid programs to international control. The United States, for instance, is no more likely to disengage itself from a direct aid relationship with certain developing countries than the Soviet Union is to allow the World Bank to handle its aid relations with the United Arab Republic.

In the case of some erstwhile imperial powers, moreover, there remain close cultural and economic and even defense ties with former colonies. The French, for instance, maintain such ties with certain of their former African colonies. Their desire to do so is not to be dismissed as something dictated merely by the selfish protection of their own interests. Along with the British, they have a sense of responsibility for, and a feeling of special association with, former colonies that is not by any means all selfish. African countries can benefit from this feeling of special commitment. The French and the British are not likely, therefore, to agree—nor will all the African governments wish them to agree—to direct all their aid funds into multilateral channels.

Even smaller developed countries recognize particular areas of interest and friendship and tend to single out certain countries for a special aid relationship. In the case of Canada, for instance, most of these are Commonwealth countries, with which there are historic and valued ties. The purist would argue that Canada should simply meet its aid commitments by handing over all appropriations to international agencies for fair and even-handed distribution wherever they may be needed. This sounds logical but ignores the stimulus that a country gets from accepting and discharging a responsibility in a special relationship that has nothing selfish about it. Canadians, for example, have a natural affinity for their Commonwealth friends in the Caribbean, one which has been built up by personal and business and official contacts over many decades. We find sun and warmth there during our cold winters. So why should we not get a special satisfaction out of helping to improve communications, hotels and beaches which add to their income from tourism and our enjoyment? There are some advantages, then, which come from working together bilaterally in aid and development matters that would not exist if the operations were all multilateral.

Special ties and interest with the old imperial masters are diminishing, however. The process is assisted by some of the new, independent governments, which see in the assertion of such a continuing interest, however well meaning, the threat of neo-colonialism. That is why it is important, especially for the former colonial rulers, not to try to impose aid programs or particular aid projects on a receiving country, or to bring political factors and pressures into bilateral discussions of aid and development questions. We should also avoid the approach: "Take our surplus dried skim milk even though you want a cement plant!" The tendency is not restricted to former imperial powers, and it can result in resentment, rather than any feeling of gratitude, for "aid" given in this way.

The foregoing remarks underline the importance of something that should be obvious: whatever procedure is followed, the aid relationship should be based on a genuine spirit of collaboration and partnership. Although some countries are in a position to give help and others need it, all—as we have seen—benefit from the assistance that is given. Consequently, there should be no feeling of one-sided generosity. Indeed, the spirit in which aid is offered and received, is as important as the aid itself. Less materially developed countries do not want crumbs or even a loaf tossed from the rich man's table. There should be a genuine feeling of participation on the part of the receiving nation in the aid relationship or it will not be successful; and that applies to both bilateral and multilateral aid.

It is not easy to establish or to conduct this kind of aid relationship, and the cooperation that should flow from it. As we have seen, it requires deep and sympathetic understanding on both sides as well as a willingness to give and take, to look forward not backward. An almost superhuman effort, rejecting short-range pressures and temptations in order to achieve longer-term and better results, must be made by new nations struggling ahead in the face of great obstacles. Western developed countries must help them by aid policies based on long-range considerations, for they, too, must be willing to make long-term investments and have the patience to await results.

Too much aid for development has been impetuous, uncertain, and tightly controlled. It is right that donor governments should wish to keep close watch over grants or loans to see that their utilization justifies further appropriations. But the allocation of aid for short periods, with no certainty that it will be continued and too much red tape, often defeats its purpose. If we are to encourage the kind of over-all aid strategy which goes to the very heart of the development problem, then we must give some assurance to the recipients that they can count on external support for more than a year at a time. There should be no blank checks, of course. But there must also be some confidence in continuity of aid if there is to be effective long-range planning. Developing governments will be in a far better position to take the long view of their problems and their plans if they have some assurance of a flow of external aid over a reasonable period of time to supplement their own efforts, while understanding that the flow would be reduced or even cease if the resources so transferred were not used for constructive purposes.

The instinct of Western legislators to prefer annual appropriations is understandable. It arises from a quite proper anxiety not to waste money, as well as from the normal and constitutional requirements of annual budgeting. However, ways can be found—and in many cases are being found—to give an assurance that help will be on a longer-term basis than one year. This will make it possible, as in the case of India, to tie appropriations in with a government's own five-year plan. This is the way it should be done; the receiving country getting some assurance about a continuing aid relationship if its own performance justifies that continuity.

The principles of partnership that should underlie such

an aid relationship were summarized in the Report of our Commission, which called for:

. . . a new partnership based on an informal understanding expressing the reciprocal rights and obligations of donors and recipients. The precise arrangements will and should differ from country to country, but, broadly, aid-providers, including international organizations, should be able to expect periodic consultations in matters of economic policy central to growth, fulfillment of understandings with respect to economic performance, and efficient use of aid funds. Recipients, on the other hand, should be entitled to a prompt and reasonably steady aid flow at the level agreed and allocation of additional aid according to explicit criteria emphasizing economic performance.

Moreover, long-term development

. . . should enjoy a presumption that it will survive changes in government, short of extreme tyranny or financial irresponsibility. Development aid should not be used to serve short-term political ends.*

* *Partners in Development*, pp. 127–28.

IV

The Totality of the Problem

I have already emphasized the need to recognize the totality of development—the need to plan for cooperation covering *all* its aspects. There is much more to providing aid for the development of poorer countries than the transfer of resources, human and material, from one government directly to another or through international agencies. Development, it cannot be stressed too often, is not a simple or a single process since its planning and strategy cover many sectors of an extended and interconnected front, social, political, economic, humanitarian.

One of these sectors is trade; another is private investment; a third is the burden of foreign debt. There is also, and this is most important, the population explosion which I have already touched on, though it deserves a much more thorough examination and analysis. There is, finally, technical assistance, including personal and voluntary services, which often are as important as official technical aid. Indeed, there are other aspects of cooperation for development that I do not even mention here. I should, however, like to say a few words about those I have mentioned, the first being tra

*   *   *

I have already traced very briefly the effect of earlier trading patterns on the growth, or lack of it, of developing countries. These patterns, derived from colonial days, are still dominant. They are, basically, the exchange of raw materials for manufactures, an exchange still largely controlled by the industrial countries and, in any event, usually insufficient to secure for developing countries the foreign exchange that is necessary to remove major external constraints on their progress. Export earnings are by far the most important source for this foreign exchange, being four times as important as the flow of aid and private investment.

We are often told that it is "trade not aid" that matters most. In a sense this slogan is right, but it is misleading if it gives the impression that trade will in the near future be able to remove the necessity for "aid" to poorer developing countries. In fact, for the great majority of such countries, this will not happen for some time.

"Aid," of course, is meant to be temporary; to help reach the goal of self-sustaining growth. You are helped on the "take-off" so that you can fly on your own. The length of the period when help is needed, however, will depend to a considerable extent on whether the policies of those few countries that dominate and virtually control world trade are liberal or restrictive. If the latter, this will not only prolong the take-off, but it can also undermine or even destroy the purpose and most of the value of the aid that is given, however generous. Therefore aid and trade policies should be kept in harmony and balance. This is not always done, nor is it easy. Governments often act in a fashion where their trade policies contradict their aid policies. At times this may result from no conscious purpose; at other times it is done by design.

International commodity prices are an example of the un-
planned result. A drop of a cent or two in the price of a
primary product—a drop which might have been prevented
by stabilizing prices at reasonable levels through national
and international policies—may wipe out in a day the total
value of the aid a country receives in a year.

There could be no better way to help the economic development of low-income countries, most of whose exports
are primary products and in many cases predominantly *one*
product, than to stabilize commodity prices by international
agreement. Some success has been achieved here with certain
commodities, but the difficulties are great and the possibilities
not too encouraging. There are limitations on this kind of
international action to boost earnings from the export of
primary products.

Part of the responsibility for failure to make greater progress rests on the developing countries themselves because of
their failure to agree on production and marketing controls
as an essential part of any international agreement. Stable
and remunerative prices can only be secured by coordination
of the production plans of producing countries, providing
for an expansion of the share of the market for new and
efficient producers; by national production controls, with
special taxes; and by diversification programs to move resources into new production. Both international and domestic controls have been difficult to achieve, nor will it ever be
easy to do so.

There is the other category, in which the responsibility
for restricting imports from low-income countries is assumed
by developed countries as a matter of planned policy. Reasons
for this course are easy for a politician to understand, even
if not to justify. The financial impact of a transfer of capital

or goods or services from a rich to a poor country can be spread over all the people of the donor country. No one is hurt by it, if there is any hurt, any more than anyone else. The tax burden is spread over the whole body of taxpayers, who are not an organized pressure group, except at election time. Indeed, there are some who will benefit from the aid expenditure because, in accord with the regrettable but accepted practice of tying aid to national production, they will get orders and there will be more business and employment.

It is a very different matter when, instead of giving $100 million in grants or loans, you are asked to import from the country you wish to aid some millions of shirts that can undersell the product of domestic manufacturers who are well organized to make their views known, swiftly and powerfully, about the iniquity of this kind of competition. In such a contingency, long-range economic interest may lose out to short-run political pressure. The legislator, like the government, has then to decide which is more important: development in the Far East or votes in the Middle West; whether to act as a statesman and lose his shirt, or as a politician and keep his seat, which, of course, is where he must sit if he is to help the poor and downtrodden of the underdeveloped world. No wonder there are some who consider aid as a "softer option to trade."

It is a dilemma that I can appreciate more than most, having been an elected head of a democratic government as well as a chairman of an international development commission. Yet it is a dilemma that provides a genuine test as to whether we are really sincere in our protestations of desire to help developing countries help themselves—indeed, to free themselves from the need for any special help. The international trade situation at present is a good illustration of the need, as well as a strong argument in favor of measures to meet it by increasing imports from the developing countries, by giving certain of their imports temporary preferential treatment, and, at the very least, by removing the existing discriminations against them.

The figures tell the story. True, they show that exports from developing countries have increased 4.7 per cent annually from 1953 to 1968. Nevertheless, and this is the significant point, they grew less rapidly than did world trade as a whole. The share of world trade held by developing countries in 1953 was 27 per cent; in 1967 it was 19 per cent. In primary products, which make up the bulk of their exports, it declined over the same period from 54 per cent to 42 per cent. Moreover, the prices received very often decreased in relation to the higher prices that had to be paid for imports; the terms of trade ran against the developing countries.

There was also a significant change in the structure of exports from these countries. From 1953 to 1967 the share of foodstuffs and agricultural raw materials declined as a percentage of total exports from 60 to less than 50. The share of manufactures, minerals, and fuels rose correspondingly. It was an encouraging sign that exports of manufactures increased annually by 12.7 per cent between 1959 and 1960, and between 1965 and 1966. This holds out real promise for the future, but only if obstacles and discriminations against the importation of manufactures can be removed by developed countries.

Here again, however, the blame should not all be laid on one side. The developing countries themselves must make greater efforts to increase and diversify their exports, to reduce their dependence on imports from industrialized countries, and to rely more on trade among themselves. In 1966, developing countries imported from the developed $4.2 billion of food, $2 billion of textiles and clothing, and $18.6 billion of manufactured goods. At present they take less than 20 per cent of their imports from each other, although, of course, there is considerable regional variation. They must work harder by regional agreements and in other ways to alter this percentage.

Above all, *total* world trade must continue to expand vigorously. This expansion can only be achieved by prosperity and steady growth in the richer, industrialized countries, for it will not help the poorer countries merely to have a larger share of a declining market.

* * *

Private investment is another sector of the total assistance front that should be closely examined in its several aspects. The part it plays in the development of low-income countries can be very important, but it is very different from official "aid." The fact that private investment is included along with governmental grants and loans in the statistics of total "aid" can lead, as we have seen, to misunderstanding about the nature, as well as the burden, of "aid."

Private investment is not a burden; and if it is a gamble, then it is one undertaken by the investor. It is not "aid" in the sense that official transfers from a government are "aid." To point out this distinction does not mean that private investment may not assist the development of the receiving country. It can and does. But it is help from which both to benefit. It is nothing that is given away.

there is no difference between the investment ds in Canada or in Chile. Both may contribute omic growth of the host country. From this the investor hopes to make a profit. There is nothing wrong in that, but there is no reason why his investment should be considered as something for which he or his government should expect to receive any special gratitude. It is very doubtful, indeed, whether such an investment should be included in "aid" totals at all; or credited to a national commitment of 1 per cent, or any other percentage, of gross national product for foreign aid.

The Bible puts this kind of help—however useful it may be—in the right category in Luke 6:34, "If ye lend to them of whom ye hope to receive, what thank have ye? For sinners also lend to sinners, to receive as much again."

While all this has a bearing on the argument over the burden of "aid," it does not affect the importance of trying to increase private investment in developing countries by wise policies and attitudes on both the lending and receiving sides. As to the magnitude of such investment, the figures are revealing.

The total flow of private investment in 1968 amounted to nearly $6 billion, almost as much as official aid transfers in that year and double the private flow of 1958.

Direct corporate investment is the largest single part of this flow but also the most politically sensitive. The accumulated total of direct corporate investment was $30 billion at the end of 1966, almost half of which was in the production of petroleum and in mining. New direct corporate investment reached a figure of about $2.8 billion in 1968. Private export credits, which are also and even more dubiously classified as "aid," are substantial and growing rapidly. During 1956–58, they averaged $375 million per annum. In the period 1966–68, the figure reached an average of $1,333 million.

Bond issues, on the other hand, which were once the main

channel for foreign private investment, are now much less important. During the period 1964–68 only Israel, Mexico, and Argentina were able to float bonds, totalling more than $100 million. It is to be hoped that conditions will soon make it possible for increased purchases of the bonds of developing countries in the capital markets of developed countries.

The flow of equity capital from individual investors in developed countries is also very small and is directed mainly to a few companies in the more industrialized developing countries, such as Mexico and Brazil.

To sum up, private foreign investment can make an important contribution to development. Host countries should, therefore, on economic grounds not only refrain from discriminatory or confiscatory treatment but also adopt policies that will encourage such investment. This need not prejudice, however, their right to take steps to ensure that the foreign investment does not result in too great an outside control of their economy and its development, or in the kind of exploitation that was all too common in the past.

Developing societies, most of them suspicious and with a sense of this past exploitation, are likely to be disturbed if too large a stake in their economic future is held by corporations whose interests and hearts lie in New York, London, Brussels or Tokyo. On this point, I quote from the recent Report of Governor Nelson Rockefeller on the quality of life in the Americas:

Private investment, particularly foreign investment, is regarded with suspicion in many quarters. A great many and probably a majority of the citizens of hemisphere nations regard United States private investment as a form of exploitation or economic colonialism. There is a widespread, mistaken view that such investment takes more out of the area than it contributes to it.

Fear of domination by United States companies is expressed frequently.*

It seems clear that corporations, if only in their own interests, should make sure that their foreign subsidiaries identify themselves to the maximum possible extent with the host country, respect both its sovereignty and its sensitivities, act as good corporate citizens, and train and employ local people at ever-rising levels of business responsibility, thereby communicating a feeling of national participation and responsibility in the operation made possible by foreign capital. They should also be prepared, in appropriate circumstances, to share ownership with local governments or business interests.

The investor has the right to insist on equitable treatment without unfair discrimination; and his home government has the right to help him secure this, though it should try to keep aid policy and investment disputes separate. Neither has the right to ask for more than this or to make profit the only consideration in helping to develop the resources of a host country.

In the best of circumstances, however, there will be difficulty and there may be distrust, which will naturally be more likely to occur on the receiving side. The complaints on both sides were well summarized by Edwin Martin, Chairman of Development Assistance Committee, in his 1968 report to the OECD, as follows:

Companies often complain about certain aspects of host country policies—such as uncertainty about the basic attitude of government towards private foreign investment, undue restrictions on

* *The Rockefeller Report on the Americas: The Official Report of a United States Presidential Mission for the Western Hemisphere*, by Nelson A. Rockefeller, The New York Times Edition (Chicago: Quadrangle Books, 1969), p. 89.

repatriation of profits or on the use of expatriate personnel, discrimination in favor of domestic (especially publicly-owned) enterprises, administrative interference and delays, price controls and other restrictions. Host countries, in turn, complain about lack of integration in the domestic economy, failure to conform to the host country programmes for improving its economic position, excessive profit expectations, failure to reinvest an adequate part of the profits, lack of interest in promoting exports, reliance on foreign supplies of raw materials and components as well as personnel rather than on domestic resources, absence of local research and training programmes.*

These complaints can be, and are increasingly being, resolved, but this requires a very different attitude on the part of foreign investors than that which was so prevalent in the "good old days" of colonial exploitation.

There are those who believe that transfers of capital, official *or* private, should be made only for the development of those economies which are organized on a free enterprise and competitive basis. I have already mentioned this opinion in reference to "conditions" attached to aid.

We in North America are the products of this kind of competitive development, and, in terms of economic growth, we haven't done badly. Therefore, it is argued, developing countries should grow as we grew, by following the principles and practices of free enterprise and the market economy.

Here again, however, we are in danger of assuming that what worked for us in the past should now work satisfactorily in very different conditions for other countries.

* Edwin M. Martin, *Development Assistance: Efforts and Policies of the Members of the Development Assistance Committee; 1968 Review* (Paris: OECD, 1968), p. 108.

The history of many developing countries has given them a deep and understandable prejudice not only against certain kinds of private investment from outside, but against the whole free enterprise, capitalist background of that investment, which has usually had the support of foreign governments behind it.

This is one reason why so many of the governments in the newly independent developing countries are socialist, to a greater or less extent. Their leaders may have found socialist views on colonial relations politically congenial when they went to the London School of Economics or Columbia or the Sorbonne. They may believe that their people have been exploited by free enterprise capitalism. They also know that, in any event, very poor countries do not have the resources to afford free competition. Free enterprise produces great rewards for those who are free and enterprising enough to secure them. It can spark progress and growth; yet it is often an expensive process which can be afforded only by countries with sufficient resources to take risks and make some mistakes. A country with minimal wealth and production, which must deal with much more powerful countries, inevitably requires more government intervention and control than does a stronger country. In the United States, free enterprise is powerful enough to take chances and to resist foreign economic pressures, with occasional Congressional assistance. But even confirmed laissez-faire economists will admit that the governments of weak and poor countries must select with care the kind of economic development on which they will embark, and the foreign investment which they will encourage. They cannot leave it entirely to the promoter, to the market, or to the investor. If the need for the conservation and direction of scarce resources makes for socialism, in one or another of its various forms, it should not be considered as a reason either for discouraging investment in that country when other conditions make it possible and desirable, or for cutting off official aid flows.

If a host country, however, discriminates unfairly against outside investment or resorts to nationalization by outright confiscation, then a different situation is created and an aid or investment relationship becomes virtually impossible.

Although a deteriorating political and economic climate in some developing countries has hindered or even prevented foreign investment, in most cases such investment is still desired and sought and is being secured. A better understanding of both its importance and its responsibility to the host country is evolving, which should help to avoid political difficulties and to maximize economic benefits. Between the investing and receiving side a better relationship is developing.

*   *   *

A third important aspect of development, one associated with investment, is the heavy and increasing burden of debt. In some developing countries the burden is almost unbearable. The fact that, in a few cases, it is a problem largely of their own creation through extravagant and even irresponsible borrowing practices in the past does not help much, especially as, in those earlier years, the extravagances were not often discouraged by the lending government or corporation.

Whatever the origin of the problem, repayment of interest

and amortization on debts previously incurred has become in many cases a serious obstacle to development, one that could also reduce or even prevent future loans. Again, the figures tell the story.

In June 1968, the total external public debt of the developing countries was $47.5 billion, which represented an annual average increase of 14 per cent in the preceding ten years. Export credits, which have also been increasing rapidly, would bring the total figure up to more than $50 billion. As a result of this increase, the proportion of loans to grants-in-aid flows has gone up from 13 per cent to 50 per cent in the last ten years.

In addition, the terms of official loans have hardened, from an average rate of 3.1 per cent in 1964 to 3.3 per cent in 1968. World Bank loans, which were as low as $4\frac{1}{4}$ per cent in the late 1940s, reached 7 per cent in that year. Loan maturities were down from 28.4 years to 24.8 years.

This hardening of terms has resulted in an increasingly heavy reverse flow of funds, to the point where in a few countries it equals, or exceeds, the capital inflow. In 1967, the total reverse flow was $4.7 billion, which represented an annual average increase in the previous ten years of 17 per cent. The present ratio of debt-servicing to new loans is 87 per cent in Latin America, 73 per cent in African states, 40 per cent in Southeast Asia and the Middle East. If the present trend continues, in five years that ratio will reach more than 100 per cent in many developing countries.

The debt situation is serious, and relief must be provided, yet this must be done in a way which will not destroy a country's credit.

The Report of the Commission on International Develop-

ment points out that there are several measures which can
and should be taken:

• Debt relief operations, which may be required, should avoid
the need for repeated reschedulings and seek to re-establish a
realistic basis for development finance.

• The terms of all official development assistance loans should
henceforth provide for interest of no more than 2 per cent, a
maturity of between 25 and 40 years, and a grace period of 7
to 10 years. (One of the Commissioners dissented from this
recommendation.)

• Developed countries should consider debt relief a legitimate
form of aid and permit new loans to be used to refinance debt
payments in order to reduce the need for full-scale debt negoti-
ations.

*   *   *

A final aspect of development which I want to mention—I
have already referred to it in another context—is technical
assistance: the transfer of human resources, skills, and know-
how from developed to developing countries. This kind of
assistance is both official and voluntary. The latter, voluntary
help, comes through a great variety of national and international organizations, without as much coordination of
their activities as is desirable. It involves many thousands of
dedicated workers and plays a more important part in
cooperation for development, both quantitatively and qual-
itatively, than is often appreciated.

Official technical assistance, in one form or another,
amounted in money terms to about $1.5 billion in 1968,
having increased at a rate of about 10 per cent a year. If
that rate of increase is continued—which is, I admit, unlikely—there could be something like 250,000 men and

women working by 1975 in developing countries in public programs alone.

There have been some notable achievements in this important activity, but, as might be expected with such rapid expansion into new fields, there have been some failures and shortcomings. At times, technical assistance has not been adequately integrated into capital assistance, or directed clearly enough to development. Local costs have often been too high, while the quality of performance, on both the donor and the recipient side, has at times left something to be desired.

In the vitally important field of education, not enough has been done by innovation and experimentation to help develop educational systems and procedures that are relevant to local needs and conditions. Traditional methods of teaching are occasionally buttressed instead of being scrapped. There is not enough aid for research and development, to be conducted wherever possible in the country or region itself and always aimed at local requirements and possibilities. If I expand on this last point somewhat, the reason is that the vast economic disparities between the wealthy industrialized nations and the poorer less-developed nations are in large measure a by-product of the scientific and technological changes that have taken place in the world since the advent of the industrial revolution. Yet the forces which have done so much to create this gap continue to operate to widen it.

It is estimated that 98 per cent of all expenditures on research and development are made in the industrialized nations, which already have the scientific and technological know-how and infrastructure that enable them to maintain high rates of growth. Furthermore, the distribution of research effort in the industrialized countries is largely irrelevant to the problems of the developing ones. Some 50 per cent of the research effort of the developed countries, for instance, is devoted to problems of defense, space, and atomic energy, and less than 1 per cent to problems that concern the poorer, developing countries.

It will require a deliberate change of policy on the part of the industrialized nations to redress this imbalance by redirecting, as foreign aid, a greater portion of the total scientific and technological research effort to development problems. It is estimated that, to date, less than one-half of 1 per cent of total aid flows have been related to such research and development.

The Commission proposes such a change by its recommendation that aid suppliers should devote 5 per cent of their expenditures for research and development to projects specifically related to problems of developing countries, half of which should be used in those countries.

In any such change of policy intended to bring about a greater application of science and technology to the development of low-income countries, it is important that there should be careful planning and wise selection of particular fields and projects for assistance. In this connection, an agency such as the International Development Research Center, which is expected shortly to be set up by Canada as part of its aid program, should be of great value. A relatively small headquarters' group in this Centre will work in close communication with other international agencies to identify specific development problems susceptible to solution through the application of science and technology. Once a specific problem area has been identified, it will organize programs designed to concentrate resources on the search for solutions and will seek the assistance of other institutions, private and official, to implement the program. Agencies and individuals in the developing countries will also be closely involved. For example, a program designed to improve the varieties of seeds might be carried out principally by a university in a "rich" country, but could also include individual research projects carried out by Departments of Agriculture and by institutes in developing countries. The Centre would be empowered to provide necessary financial support.

One of the principal deficiencies now existing in international cooperation for development is the lack of any centralized system for assimilation, storage, retrieval, and dissemination of scientific and technical data. One of the tasks of the proposed Canadian Research Centre would be to provide the principal link in an international system to meet this need.

The most spectacular example to date of what can be accomplished by concentrating scientific and technological resources on the search for a solution to a particular growth and production problem is the development of the new high-yielding varieties of wheat and rice, which have made possible an agricultural revolution in Asia. The work was financed largely by the Ford and Rockefeller Foundations. With an original investment of little more than $50 million, it may well have produced more real and lasting economic benefit to developing nations than the several billions of dollars of other kinds of "aid" which they have received.

This is the kind of activity which should be greatly extended by international cooperation. It will require, however, not only financial resources but also technical assistance in the organization and selection of projects, as well as a greater emphasis on the right kind of research and development to be promoted and the wise application of its results.

Too often, assistance for study abroad—especially in the field of science and technology—has resulted in a "brain drain." Those with the skills, intelligence, and training that would enable them to give valuable service in their own countries are drawn by better opportunities and higher incomes to remain in Europe and North America, and thus are often lost forever to their homelands. One estimate even claims that almost 50 per cent of the graduate engineers of Latin America work in the United States, and that two-thirds of the health services in Britain are manned by Pakistani and Indian doctors. Rather than the massive migration of those whose human needs are greatest and which once took millions of the wretched but ambitious poor from Europe to America, it is now the elite who are able to migrate, leaving behind the mass of their own people in poverty and stagnation. This is a form of technical assistance in reverse and is becoming a problem of growing significance.

We should not forget that, while technical assistance requires large funds, it needs even more, as I have already pointed out, the right kind of people with a right understanding of the local problems they are helping to solve and an appreciation of the life and culture and conditions of the country in which they are working. The occasional failure to face up to the human requirements of technical assistance is reflected in the controversies, which used to be popular a few years ago at conference round-tables and in letters to the editor, over the qualifications and the circumstances of those who went abroad on aid missions or as technical experts. It will always be possible, of course, to find some second-rate people serving abroad. There may also be a few "ugly" types without much conscience, as well as the quiet and more pleasant kind with generosity and conscience but with not enough imagination, understanding, or adaptability for the sensitive nature of an assignment far from home and normal life. Sometimes we get a caricature of both types by returning tourists, or even from politicians who have been traveling abroad. It would be very nice for all of us if we could, as we did in the past, merely put our few pennies in the missionary box each Sunday and let a few dedicated people go out into remote places and, on our behalf, save souls, cure bodies, and find their own reward in heaven. Such people are still going into jungles on the same devoted and unselfish service. But we now need in addition to them thousands of engineers, teachers, and technicians with technical skills and the understanding heart, who are not only good in their own fields but also have the human qualities required.

Handicaps imposed by different backgrounds of culture and conditions can usually be overcome or mitigated by people who care enough about what they are doing. Nevertheless, to avoid the human difficulties which are at times inevitable in even the best of assistance from outside, local people should be trained to take over as soon as possible the skilled and technical work done by outsiders, however well it may be done.

Patience and dedication and understanding, then, as well as technical skills, are required both on the contributing and on the receiving side. Nevertheless, whenever East meets West, there are bound to be personality and background difficulties. These do not necessarily vanish when the aid relationship is under the aegis of the United Nations or some other international or voluntary organization.

I recall a situation arising out of a bilateral Colombo Plan project in which Canadians and Pakistanis worked together in a remote region near the Afghan frontier. There were inevitably some differences of viewpoint as to how the project should be carried out. The closeness of the unaccustomed contact inevitably created some friction between men whose backgrounds were so different. The Canadians, in conditions which at home would be considered not too easy, were able, however, to maintain a standard and a way of living which contrasted rather starkly with that of some of the local people. So, naturally, a few problems and jealousies developed. Indeed, at one time in the earlier stages of the project, these reached proportions which threatened its continuance. There were faults, of course, on both sides. Instead of allowing matters to boil, a conference was called in Ottawa at which Pakistani and Canadian engineers and government officials talked the whole thing over. Although much of the talk was about technical matters, a good deal involved the easing process of getting things off their chests. The result was wonderfully beneficial. The problems did not, of course, evaporate, but they were reduced. There was a new understanding of each other's difficulties which carried through the succeeding years. This is only one illustration of a process and an approach that is essential if technical assistance is to be as valuable for development purposes as it has on so many occasions shown itself to be.

V

Proposals and Conclusions

I would like to conclude these lectures by brief but specific references to certain recommendations of the Report of our Commission, even if this means some repetition.

There are sixty-eight formal recommendations and several less formal suggestions in the Report. Their general objective is to support and strengthen cooperation for development and to give a clearer purpose and greater coherence to "aid" strategy. To this end there are recommendations to increase the quantity of "aid" and improve its quality and its utilization, to emphasize the fundamental importance of the concept of partnership in the total aid relationship, to increase the export trade of developing countries and promote sound foreign investment, to make aid organization and administration more effective and strengthen its multilateral element, to increase the value of technical assistance, and, last —but very far from least—to deal with the population explosion.

In the first chapter of its Report, the Commission summarizes its general conclusions, and I do not think I can do better here than to summarize that summary.

The record of economic growth in developing countries

over the last two decades is a good one and should be a source of confidence, rather than discouragement, for the future.

This record shows that, where there has been a resolute national purpose and a sincere effort on the part of developing countries, economic growth has resulted, and external aid has helped to sustain and accelerate that growth.

When failures have occurred, these have been largely due to political weakness, or instability, in developing countries, when governments have subordinated the known and necessary needs of long-term development for more immediate and selfish political goals, or when "aid" commitments have been inadequate or not carried out. Reversals in other sectors of development, such as trade, have also contributed to failures.

While "aid" has been of great importance, the problem of development, in all its aspects, can be solved only by each country itself. Nothing of lasting significance can be achieved without national drive, national sacrifice, and national leadership.

The technical means are now available—if the political will is strong enough—to create a world of expanding opportunity for all, without today's abject poverty and the debilitating disparities in economic and social standards that now exist between nations.

This, however, will not be achieved without active and constructive international cooperation for world development, based on a partnership which should be insulated, as much as possible, from international politics.

Economic growth must be balanced against social goals, something that can be done only by the developing countries.

When it is not done, economic growth will be nullified by social weakness and division.

There can be no single strategy of development, but there must be agreement on basic principles, and programs should be welded into a coherent and coordinated system.

Much has been learned about the problems of cooperation for development. What is necessary now is to apply what has been learned with a clearer sense of purpose, more accurate assessment of needs, and a closer relationship between aid commitments and aid performance on both the donor and receiver sides.

The proportion of aid through multilateral channels should be increased, and the international agencies used for this purpose must provide leadership and efficient administration.

The total volume of aid should be increased to 1 per cent of the gross national product of the wealthy countries, a goal to be met by 1975. In view of the special need for, and declining flow of, official assistance and concessional finance, particular importance is attached to a separate target for official development transfers of 0.70 per cent of gross national product, also to be reached by 1975.

Donors and recipients should join in an effort to rationalize and simplify existing cumbersome procedures. There should be a combined attack on the practice of tying aid to purchases in donor countries, which now reduces the value of aid and distorts the channels of world trade. Greater attention should be paid to the need for program, as opposed to project, aid.

Technical assistance should be more adequately integrated with capital assistance, and be made more relevant to local conditions, especially in the fields of education, research, and development.

Mutually beneficial private capital flows should be increased, but this must be done in such a way as to recognize the legitimate interest of developing countries in maintaining maximum economic independence.

In view of the problem of mounting debts, some repayment schedules will have to be rearranged in order to restore the framework for orderly and dynamic development. Debt relief has an important part to play in aid strategy. Official development loans should be provided at rates of interest no higher than 2 per cent, with grace periods of seven to ten years, and maturities of twenty-five to forty years.

The development of poorer countries requires a continued expansion of world trade in which the developing countries should have a larger share. This requires that the trade policies of developed countries should be modified in favor of imports from the less developed ones. Trade between the developing countries themselves, both on a global and a regional basis, should be encouraged.

Population growth must be controlled so that it does not thwart social and economic progress.

*   *   *

I would also like to make a somewhat more than capsule reference to proposals in our Report dealing with the organization and administration of aid programs—something that I have mentioned only incidentally in these lectures, though it is of obvious importance.

The strategy of aid must be related to the total concept of development, and not separately to its various parts. This is particularly necessary in the organization and administration of aid, which is becoming more complex, both nationally and internationally. It should be simplified. I know how difficult this will be, and I know that it would be folly to expect total efficiency in something so complicated and which touches on so many aspects of government and of intergovernmental relations. But improvement should be possible. Indeed, it has already taken place in recent years, though much remains to be done.

Multilateral agencies should be strengthened. Existing procedures, including national procedures, are too cumbersome, too slow-moving, and there is too much overlapping. There should be a closer coordination of aid activities between governments and international agencies. This is even more important in the field than at headquarters, though the profusion of agencies often lacks direction and coherence at the top.

All the components of aid, bilateral and multilateral, should be brought into a closer relationship with each other through a new international framework designed for this purpose. The Commission has, therefore, proposed, and I consider the proposal to be most important, that the President of the World Bank should invite to a conference, to be held in 1970, the heads of appropriate organs of the United Nations, heads of multilateral agencies, regional development banks, and U.N. coordinating bodies, as well as representatives of donor and recipient governments. The conference would discuss the creation of improved coordinating machinery through a council on the highest level, which would be capable of relating aid and development policies to other relevant areas of foreign economic policy, and of making standardized assessments of development performance, as well as clear, regular, and authoritative estimates of

aid requirements. Such a council would also be able to provide balanced and impartial reviews both of the aid policies
and programs of donor governments and of the aid and
development performance of recipients. It should bring
about a more constructive and acceptable dialogue, which
should lead to a closer and better relationship between the
transfer of aid resources and their utilization—something
which I have stressed so often as especially important. This
monitoring of performance, for that is what it would be,
would be done by an international body which must reflect
in its representation and operation both sides of the aid relationship.

There would be new machinery, then, at the top, decision-
making level to cover the whole development front. On the
agency and operational level, there are already consortia and
consultative groups of donors and recipients, which have
worked well. They should be strengthened and new ones,
where required, should be set up which will also reflect this
principle of dual representation, responsibility, and operation.

The World Bank, or some other appropriate existing
agency, should provide the necessary technical reporting
services for such reviewing agencies. The World Bank and
the International Monetary Fund should also adopt procedures in countries where both operate for preparing unified
country assessments and giving expert and policy advice.

The International Development Association, the "soft loan
window" of the World Bank, should play an increasingly
important role in the whole development system. To this
end, it should be given greater financial resources—and for
a longer period than one year. Among other things, it could
formulate broad criteria to govern the allocation of concessional financing for development in order to offset some

of the more glaring inequities which now exist in aid distribution.

A key agency in the development process is the United Nations Development Program (UNDP), under the tireless, experienced, and devoted leadership of Paul Hoffman. It is the specific purpose of the UNDP, in Mr. Hoffman's words, "to help convert the latent potential [of developing countries] into fuller productivity, particularly by pre-investment surveys and technical assistance." That this potential exists is indicated by the estimate that, at present, not more than 20 per cent of the natural resources and 10 per cent of the human productive capabilities of the developing countries are being fully utilized.

The UNDP is now the largest source of pre-investment assistance. Current commitments for pre-investment and technical assistance amount to $129 million. By 1968, over $2 billion in follow-up investments had been stimulated by pre-investment activities, supported by the UNDP.

If multilateral aid is increased, as recommended by our Commission, the work and responsibilities of the UNDP would be expanded. In consequence, its organization and administration and its relations with other agencies should be so ordered as to enable it to take on these new and enlarged activities with maximum effectiveness.

*   *   *

I have attempted to indicate briefly the views and proposals of the Commission on International Development. I am very conscious of the fact, however, that, even if governments considered these proposals wise and implemented them, and if, as a result, there were a new and better aid relationship with a wise and well-administered strategy for total development, there would still be difficulties and problems. This is inevitable in the effort to build a healthy and desirable aid relationship based on partnership between materially rich and poor nations in an increasingly interdependent, swiftly changing world—a relationship which touches at so many points on complex and sensitive political and economic matters within and between nations.

I can only repeat that such an international effort cannot succeed unless there are tolerance, sympathy, and understanding on each side. These, I realize, are not qualities that can be taken for granted in relations between states, even in normal circumstances—far from it. They will certainly not exist in an aid relationship unless there is a very clear appreciation by the developing countries, which shows itself in policy and action, of what is required from them for self-sustaining growth as the foundation for self-reliant and total national development.

The list of such requirements is long. I do not apologize for mentioning again some of its main components at the end of these lectures. There must be

- Political stability, without which there can be no steady and orderly development
- Social progress based on social justice and human rights
- Integrity and efficiency in government
- Financial and economic policies which do not sacrifice long-range national objectives to immediate political pressures or ambitions
- The efficient allocation of domestic resources for development, with rates of savings and investment that are as high as possible

ese are only some of the requirements for the kind of

development policy which warrants and should secure cooperation and assistance from outside.

Even when these requirements are accepted in principle, their implementation will often be frustrated by

- Insurmountable social and cultural obstacles to the necessary reforms
- Failure to save and invest sufficiently for growth, because people are so poor that everything goes to mere survival
- The lack of political will, of the resolution to make the effort and the sacrifices necessary for success (Failure here is often due to the feeling that the problems to be faced seem so intractable as to defy solution; so why bother?)
- An acute shortage of technical skill and know-how
- Too high a rate of population increase
- Modernization of agriculture, without sufficient regard to local conditions
- Industrialization artificially or uneconomically forced
- An educational system not directed to local needs and possibilities, which include the development at home of technology, science, and know-how
- Trade and fiscal policies which do not provide for a sound and steady increase in exports

These, then, are some of the requirements that must be met, some of the obstacles that must be overcome by the developing countries if cooperation for world development is to succeed. Any country that is trying to meet and overcome them has, I repeat, the right to expect and receive the material help and the understanding cooperation of those who are economically more advanced and richer in material things. Its right is our obligation. It is important to both sides that this obligation should be discharged. Indeed, the "aid" is as mutual as the obligation is general, and the results, for better or for worse, will be universal.

We have now finished a decade which began with the all but total liquidation of the old imperialism and ended with man on the moon. It was a time of troubles and problems but also of great technical achievement—some of it bearing hope for the future, some menacing. The next decade may be an even more difficult period of tension and crisis. Things are still changing and with ever more bewildering speed, and change normally means disruption. If we are to guide the forces of change rather than be mastered by them, we must be wise and far-sighted in our national and international policies. One test of that wisdom and far-sightedness will be what we do about international cooperation to bring about more even growth and development over the whole world. We would be foolish, and worse, if we now defaulted on this novel and noble adventure in cooperation, which could have such far-reaching implications for the future. There is no cause, yet, to conclude that we will do so, to cry doom and show gloom. The "crisis of development" is a very real one, but it can be overcome—not with timidity or despair but with sensible realism, which insists we look risks and dangers in the face.

The 1970s may bring crises, but they also offer vast opportunities for positive and creative action in the international development field. We have the means, if we have the will, to act. The opportunities before us should make us bold, not beaten, for our capacity to exploit them is almost limitless. If the technological skill which took man into outer space can be linked with moral awareness and recognition

of the urgent and practical need for international cooperation, we can bring a better life to all mankind.

This is the light.

The dark comes from our fears and our hates, our wrong
priorities and our rooted prejudices, the destructive use to
which we put so much of our technology, the poisoning and
polluting of our environment, weariness, and a declining
public commitment to new international responsibilities.

With will and work, the light can overcome the dark. An
important move to this end, and one which would be a test
of our resolve, would be to strengthen international cooperation for development, to work toward a goal where world
welfare is as normal as world conflict, and world responsibility as normal as world discord.

We are at a moment in human destiny when new opportunities and new hopes can be held out to the submerged
and impoverished billions. The gates of the future are not
closed. They are ajar; they will respond to a determined
push. But we cannot push if we lack the will, though we have
strength, materially, in abundance. Two hundred years of
technological and capital growth have placed at the disposal
of the richer countries unprecedented resources, which grow,
on the average, by 4 or 5 per cent a year. We know so much
more now about the problems of world development than
before, and knowledge is a first stage essential to doing something about them. Compared with the innocence with which
the development process was approached only two decades
ago, sophistication and understanding are now the order of
the day. A more careful study of facts and needs has taken
the place of earlier overoptimism based on illusions and ignorance. We have made great steps forward in understanding what is actually happening. We have also made great

steps forward in understanding what now has to be done. These are important gains that have occurred in the last two decades, for, as I have just said, more knowledge and greater understanding are the foundation for better work and greater progress.

What a tragedy it would be if we slackened, faltered, and gave up at this time because only the will is lacking!

What a triumph, if the seriousness of the challenge were met by the greatness of the response!

Index

COUNCIL ON FOREIGN RELATIONS

Officers and Directors

John J. McCloy, *Chairman of the Board*
Henry M. Wriston, *Honorary President*
Grayson Kirk, *President*
Frank Altschul, *Vice-President & Secretary*
David Rockefeller, *Vice-President*
Gabriel Hauge, *Treasurer*
George S. Franklin, Jr., *Executive Director*

Hamilton Fish Armstrong
William P. Bundy
William A. M. Burden
Arthur H. Dean
Douglas Dillon
Hedley Donovan
William C. Foster
Caryl P. Haskins
Joseph E. Johnson
Henry R. Labouisse

Bill D. Moyers
Alfred C. Neal
James A. Perkins
Lucian W. Pye
Philip D. Reed
Robert V. Roosa
Charles M. Spofford
Cyrus Vance
Carroll L. Wilson

PUBLICATIONS

FOREIGN AFFAIRS (quarterly), edited by Hamilton Fish Armstrong.
THE UNITED STATES IN WORLD AFFAIRS (annual), by Richard P. Stebbins.

Documents on American Foreign Relations (annual), by Richard P. Stebbins with the assistance of Elaine P. Adam.

Political Handbook and Atlas of the World, 1970, edited by Richard P. Stebbins and Alba Amoia (1970).

The Crisis of Development, by Lester B. Pearson (1970).

The Great Powers and Africa, by Waldemar A. Nielsen (1969).

A New Foreign Policy for the United States, by Hans J. Morgenthau (1969).

Middle East Politics: The Military Dimension, by J. C. Hurewitz (1969).

The Economics of Interdependence: Economic Policy in the Atlantic Community, by Richard N. Cooper (1968).

How Nations Behave: Law and Foreign Policy, by Louis Henkin (1968).

The Insecurity of Nations, by Charles W. Yost (1968).

Prospects for Soviet Society, edited by Allen Kassof (1968).

The American Approach to the Arab World, by John S. Badeau (1968).

U.S. Policy and the Security of Asia, by Fred Greene (1968).

Negotiating with the Chinese Communists: The U.S. Experience, by Kenneth T. Young (1968).

From Atlantic to Pacific: A New Interocean Canal, by Immanuel J. Klette (1967).

Tito's Separate Road: America and Yugoslavia in World Politics, by John C. Campbell (1967).

U.S. Trade Policy: New Legislation for the Next Round, by John W. Evans (1967).

Trade Liberalization Among Industrial Countries: Objectives and Alternatives, by Bela Balassa (1967).

The Chinese People's Liberation Army, by Brig. General Samuel B. Griffith II U.S.M.C. (ret.) (1967).

The Artillery of the Press: Its Influence on American Foreign Policy, by James Reston (1967).

Atlantic Economic Cooperation: The Case of the O.E.C.D., by Henry G. Aubrey (1967).

TRADE, AID AND DEVELOPMENT: The Rich and Poor Nations, by John Pincus (1967).

BETWEEN TWO WORLDS: Policy, Press and Public Opinion on Asian-American Relations, by John Hohenberg (1967).

THE CONFLICTED RELATIONSHIP: The West and the Transformation of Asia, Africa and Latin America, by Theodor Geiger (1966).

THE ATLANTIC IDEA AND ITS EUROPEAN RIVALS, by H. van B. Cleveland (1966).

EUROPEAN UNIFICATION IN THE SIXTIES: From the Veto to the Crisis, by Miriam Camps (1966).

THE UNITED STATES AND CHINA IN WORLD AFFAIRS, by Robert Blum, edited by A. Doak Barnett (1966).

THE FUTURE OF THE OVERSEAS CHINESE IN SOUTHEAST ASIA, by Lea A. Williams (1966).

THE CONSCIENCE OF THE RICH NATIONS: The Development Assistance Committee and the Common Aid Effort, by Seymour J. Rubin (1966).

ATLANTIC AGRICULTURAL UNITY: Is it Possible?, by John O. Coppock (1966).

TEST BAN AND DISARMAMENT: The Path of Negotiation, by Arthur H. Dean (1966).

COMMUNIST CHINA's ECONOMIC GROWTH AND FOREIGN TRADE, by Alexander Eckstein (1966).

POLICIES TOWARD CHINA: Views from Six Continents, edited by A. M. Halpern (1966).

THE AMERICAN PEOPLE AND CHINA, by A. T. Steele (1966).

INTERNATIONAL POLITICAL COMMUNICATION, by W. Phillips Davison (1965).

MONETARY REFORM FOR THE WORLD ECONOMY, by Robert V. Roosa (1965).

ALTERNATIVE TO PARTITION: For a Broader Conception of America's Role in Europe, by Zbigniew Brzezinski (1965).

THE TROUBLED PARTNERSHIP: A Re-Appraisal of the Atlantic Alliance, by Henry A. Kissinger (1965).